Pacific Palate

PACIFIC PALATE

FOOD ARTISANS OF VANCOUVER ISLAND AND THE GULF ISLANDS

REVISED AND UPDATED

DON GENOVA

FOREWORD BY MARGARET GALLAGHER

TouchWood Editions
Touchwoodeditions.com

Copy edited by Warren Layberry
Proofread by Senica Maltese
Original Cover template by Colin Parks with design updates by Sydney Barnes
Original Interior template by Lara Minja with design updates by Sydney Barnes
Maps by Eric Leinberger
Image Credits on page 269

CATALOGUING DATA AVAILABLE FROM LIBRARY AND ARCHIVES CANADA
ISBN 9781771514262 (softcover)
ISBN 9781771514279 (electronic)

TouchWood Editions gratefully acknowledges that the land on which we live and work is within the traditional territories of the Lkwungen (Esquimalt and Songhees), Malahat, Pacheedaht, Scia'new, T'Sou-ke and W̱SÁNEĆ (Pauquachin, Tsartlip, Tsawout, Tseycum) peoples.

We acknowledge the financial support of the Government of Canada through the Canada Book Fund, and the province of British Columbia through the Book Publishing Tax Credit.

This book was produced using FSC®-certified, acid-free papers, processed chlorine free, and printed with soya-based inks.

Printed in China

29 28 27 26 25 1 2 3 4 5

Dedicated to my dear sister Cathy, a wonderful cook who introduced me to the wonders of a roast leg of lamb and shared travels with me around the world in search of new taste experiences.

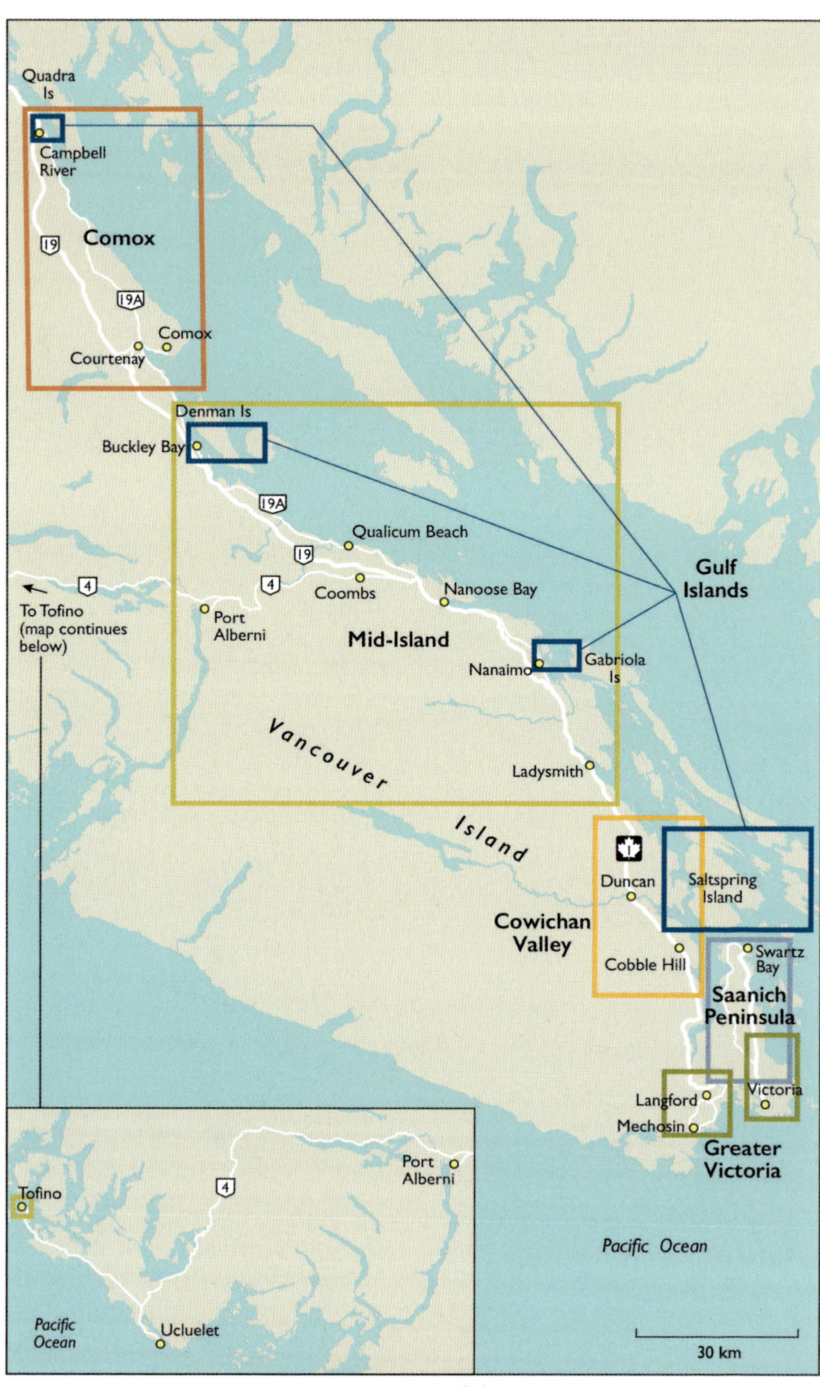

Quadra Is
Campbell River
Comox
19
19A
Comox
Courtenay
Denman Is
Buckley Bay
19A
Qualicum Beach
19
4
4
Coombs
Nanoose Bay
To Tofino (map continues below)
Port Alberni
Mid-Island
Gulf Islands
Gabriola Is
Nanaimo
Vancouver Island
Ladysmith
Duncan
Saltspring Island
Cowichan Valley
Cobble Hill
Swartz Bay
Saanich Peninsula
Langford
Victoria
Mechosin
Greater Victoria
Pacific Ocean
30 km
Tofino
Port Alberni
4
Pacific Ocean
Ucluelet

CONTENTS

FOREWORD

The smell of fresh coffee and fresh bread fills the air at True Grain Bakery in Cowichan Bay. It's a sunny summer morning and Don Genova has snagged us a cozy wooden booth, the table laden with gooey cinnamon buns, golden croissants, hearty muffins, and a brownie for later, because, well, he knows about my deep love of anything chocolate. But before we tuck in, Don takes a moment to turn me and my partner's attention to the handsome flour mill that holds a place of honour in the bustling bakery, gently illuminated behind a sparkling clean glass window.

With great enthusiasm, Don tells us that the treats we're about to enjoy were made from locally grown Red Fife wheat, which was milled into flour in this very room. He introduces us to the proud bakery owner, and tells us the story of this special place, which is clearly a local hub. Don points out some of the cheeses and jams in the shop, and tells us who made them and why. Which makes this breaking of bread together all the more delicious. And we've earned it, because we've taken two ferries and pedalled plenty of kilometres to get here.

It's July 2008 and my partner and I are in the middle of a DIY culinary bike tour of southern Vancouver Island and some nearby Gulf Islands. Our mission is simple: eat and drink delicious things made locally and meet some of the people who made them. In the pre-smart phone era, our main navigation aid is an illustrated winery map we found in a BC Ferry brochure rack earlier that spring and decided to follow on a whim. And because it's 2008, there aren't a heck of a lot of destinations or details on the simple map, but we're confident we can cobble together an interesting itinerary. Because we have a secret weapon. And his name is Don Genova.

Like countless others, I first met Don on the radio, long before I was lucky enough to meet him in person. As an avid CBC listener, I particularly loved his weekly "Pacific Palate" feature, where he introduced us to an ever-changing menu of chefs, farmers, and makers. He shared the latest food trends as well as culinary traditions from the diverse communities that make up BC. I listened with envy whenever he brought in a tasty sample for *Early Edition* host Rick Cluff, who clearly looked forward to Don's visits. A few years later, when I was lucky to find myself working at the *Early Edition*, I made a point of coming into the office extra early if there was even a slim chance to try some of the goodies Don had to share.

As delicious as those dishes were, what Don really nourished was a sense of community, and an understanding that food tells stories. He championed the importance of knowing where your food comes from, and shone a spotlight on local growers and makers. And because food brings people together, Don and I quickly became friends. Later, when he moved from Vancouver to Cobble Hill, we kept in touch.

Which is how I found myself eating a brownie for breakfast in Cowichan Bay (I couldn't resist), fresh on the heels of watching a local cheese maker in action, with a plan to check out a really great ice cream shop later in the day, and maybe visit a local cidery where we could also get some excellent brick-oven pizza. All of these have been suggested by Don Genova. And there are even more ideas, which he enthusiastically jots down on a piece of paper for us. I know how lucky I am to have Don's expertise to open my eyes and my tastebuds to the incredible bounty that is his backyard, and it crosses my mind that Don should write a book.

Skip ahead to 2014, and he has indeed written a book. *The Food Artisans of Vancouver Island and the Gulf Islands* is a delicious tribute to the region, and a way for anyone to access Don's wealth of knowledge. (You don't have to ride your bike to his house and camp in the basement.)

Since then, local bounty has continued to multiply, with new makers and growers cropping up all over the region, producing everything from gin to tea to pickles to cheese. Things have inevitably changed since that first edition, with some makers closing up shop in the face of economic pressures, which makes resources like this even more vital in getting the word out about local producers. Don has kept up with it all, which leads to the updated edition you now hold in your hand. There's even an expanded chocolate section. If my partner and I were to do that bike trip again, Don's book would keep us on the road for weeks. But what a delicious ride it would be.

Margaret Gallagher
Host of CBC's North by Northwest

INTRODUCTION

When I first came to Vancouver Island as a typical tourist, I made the same vow I'm sure many other visitors have probably made: "Someday I'm going to live here." Over the course of several more visits, that vow was reaffirmed many times, and finally, in 2003, I did make the move. I settled in the Cowichan Valley, a perfect base from which to explore many parts of the region. I have been lucky enough to see the island and the Gulf Islands from the air, from the water, by bicycle, on foot, and of course by car. It's a region best seen in as many ways as possible, especially when it comes to your palate. A walk in the woods yields juicy wild berries or earthy mushrooms; boating means great fishing, crabbing, and shrimping; and cycling on a hard-packed sand beach at low tides allows for scooping up oysters and digging for clams. I hop in my car to visit blueberry farms, hazelnut groves, and apple orchards. Then there are the growing numbers of farmers' markets, wineries, cideries, and distilleries. I moved to Victoria in 2015, where I have discovered some surprising food finds in very urban settings, such as wild fennel growing out of sidewalks and a neighbour who donated one of her artichoke plants to me. The plum tree in my backyard yields many baskets of European Bradshaw plums, which I dutifully jam and sauce every year.

Over my years of exploring, I have met some very special people. They are the people who take great pride in their work and display a passion for the products they create. Whether they are farmers growing fresh ingredients, cheese makers coaxing curds from fresh cow's, sheep's, or goat's milk, or chocolatiers crafting mouth-watering sweets, they all work very hard to make wonderful stuff for us to eat or drink.

The first edition of this book was written in 2014. At that time, I wrote about how our artisan culture was growing at a rapid pace. What I didn't foresee at the time was just how fast it would grow. Yes, the pandemic years of Covid-19 took a bite out of more than one food artisan; there were setbacks, there were shutdowns from which businesses just couldn't recover. On the flip side, though, because of disruptions in supply chains and an overall feeling that we all needed to support local businesses, some artisans managed to not only survive but thrive. More than ever, people care about where their food comes from and how it is produced, and they are driving the production of local cheeses, pasture-raised beef and chicken, and even sea salt from the waters around our islands. It's hard to keep track of all the farmers' markets that have popped up since the original edition, but the best way to keep up is by visiting the Island Farm Fresh website at islandfarmfresh.com. The site is brought to you by the Southern Vancouver Island Direct Farm Marketing Association, and you can find a searchable directory of some seventy farms all over south Vancouver Island.

A few other things I've noticed as the past decade flew by; the boom in social media means more artisans can get their word out about their products via whatever happens to be the trendiest platform of the day. In this book, you won't find exhaustive lists of TikTok, Threads, and X listings. I've stuck to websites, Facebook, and Instagram accounts as well as good old-fashioned addresses, e-mails, and phone numbers of businesses that welcome you getting in touch with them. The other thing I've noticed is how proud artisans are when they have a truly family-run affair. Having young blood in these businesses is a real bonus. We're not entirely past the time of kids not wanting to take over the family business, but I'm encouraged by all the young people who are taking an important role in their parents' professions. Make no mistake, however, creating a food or beverage product and promoting and selling it is hard work. But I continue to meet younger artisans over the years who have come to realize they don't want nine-to-five office jobs and don't mind getting into something they make and own themselves, even if it means getting dirty and working from dawn until after dark.

While I prefer to eat and drink food and beverages made from local ingredients, I have a far-ranging palate. I'm not going to give up coffee, lemons, olive oil, or cinnamon just because you can't produce them on Vancouver Island. That's why, in this book, I tell you where to find the best olive oils or spices from faraway countries. But keep in mind that we still produce a woefully small percentage of the food we eat on these islands, so where there is a choice, please purchase locally. You'll encourage the growth of community-owned businesses and support people who really deserve your patronage.

This book is meant to salute and share my knowledge of all the great artisans, shopkeepers, and farmers I've met during the twenty-plus years I've lived on Vancouver Island. I want to pass on their stories of how they got started and why I like their products. No snapshot in time like this book could cover all the artisans out there, so I'm asking you to trust my judgment. It's not too much of a stretch; with my eating history, I have a pretty good idea of what makes an excellent product!

HOW THIS BOOK IS ORGANIZED

In this edition the artisans are divided into six different regions. *Comox Valley*, as far north as Campbell River, *Cowichan Valley*, including Duncan, Mill Bay, Cobble Hill, Chemainus, and Shawnigan Lake, the *Gulf Islands*, *Mid-Island*, including Tofino, Ucluelet, Greater Nanaimo, Parksville, Qualicum Beach, Coombs, Port Alberni, and Ladysmith, the *Saanich Peninsula*, including Sidney and Brentwood Bay, and *Greater Victoria*, including Sooke, Metchosin, and Langford.

Each of the regions is then further split into categories such as bakeries, food products, and seafood. This book isn't designed as a typical travel guide, although you will have to travel to various corners of the island and Gulf Islands to find some of these products as they may be available only at farm-gate shops or particular retailers; others will be available at your local grocery store or through a few clicks to do a mail order on your computer. Many smaller shops will happily bring in a product for you if you can demonstrate continued demand and loyalty.

But no matter where you live or where you visit, page your way through the different sections of this book to find something good to eat or drink. And don't forget your shopping bags and coolers when you head out on "Saturday Sojourns."

A FEW WORDS ABOUT SUSTAINABILITY

Shoppers want it all these days: local, seasonal, certified organic, and sustainable. Over the past few years, the word *sustainable* has become a catchword not only for the environmental movement but also for marketers and entrepreneurs eager to hitch a ride on the desires of those who want to be more careful with their purchasing power. But what is sustainability? The definition that the David Suzuki Foundation has used comes from the 1987 United Nations World Commission on Environment and Development: sustainability is "meeting the needs of the present generations without compromising the ability of future generations to meet their needs."

For a little more detail, look at the foundation's *Sustainability within a Generation* document: "Sustainability means living within the Earth's limits. In a sustainable future, no Canadian would think twice about going outside for a walk or drinking a glass of tap water. Food would be free from pesticide residues, antibiotics, and growth hormones. Air, water, and soil would be uncontaminated by toxic substances. In a sustainable future, it would be safe to swim in every Canadian river and lake; safe to eat fish wherever they were caught. Clean, renewable energy would be generated by harnessing the sun, the wind, water, and heat of the Earth."

That's a mouthful. But look at the clues contained within the statement: "Food would be free from pesticide residues, antibiotics, and growth hormones." That's your key to seek out organic meats and produce and seafood from uncontaminated waters. What about when you see farmers advertising "no spray" or "pesticide free" produce at the farmers' markets? Well, that's not certified organic, and organic goes beyond the non-use of herbicides and pesticides. That's when your own judgment must come into play. Talk to the farmer. Ask how the vegetables were grown. Do their chickens have access to the open air? What do they eat? If you do want to eat in a more sustainable fashion as per the definition above, you need to do a little homework. It's a good idea to learn the difference between free-range and free-run, what pastured poultry is, and what the benefits of eating grass-fed beef or lamb can be.

You may come across the phrase "the 100-mile diet." It was the title of a book written by Vancouver authors J.B. McKinnon and

Alisa Smith and published in 2007. They told me they picked the figure arbitrarily out of the air. Even though they're Canadians living with the metric system, they thought the 100-mile diet sounded better than the 160-kilometre diet. The concept of looking for lower food miles (or kilometres), i.e., food that hasn't been shipped to you from great distances, is noble on the surface. The celebrated farmer/photographer/author/activist Michael Ableman of Salt Spring Island once said at a talk I attended, "I'd rather eat a non-organic bunch of broccoli grown on a farm down the street than an organic bunch of broccoli shipped in from Chile." Local is better, right? Usually.

These days you don't hear about the 100-mile diet too often. Instead, people may refer to themselves as *locavores*. You could try eating according to *foodsheds*. A foodshed can be defined as "a local bioregion that grows food for a specific population," but your personal definition may also depend on your choices regarding how and where the food is produced and how it gets to you. But is there anything wrong with eating mangoes from Mexico or drinking coffee from Panama when these products are produced by farmers paid fairly for their crops and work and transported in large quantities by boat instead of fuel-gobbling jets? People in developing countries countries are depending on us for a living as well. You'll come across many conundrums such as this when you are trying to live a more sustainable lifestyle. Choosing sustainable seafood is like shooting at a moving target. A species that was green-lighted by a monitoring agency this year may end up on the "exercise caution" or "endangered" list next year.

At the end of it all, no one can tell you exactly what the "right" choices are when it comes to the food you buy. It's up to you. Here are some of the definitions you'll come across on labels and signs while you are shopping for food.

- **Certified Organic, Transitional Organic, Organic:** Certified organic foods must be grown without the use of synthetic fertilizers and pesticides and are not genetically modified organisms. They are processed without the addition of artificial flavours and colours. All the ingredients and other processes that go into making a certified organic product must be certified organic as well. For example, a certified organic chicken must be fed certified organic chicken feed, and that feed must be produced with certified organic ingredients. A product that has been certified organic means the producer has documented and passed all the standards set by its particular certifying association when it comes to the growing, processing, packaging, storing, and shipping of its product, complete with occasional on-site inspection. The certification is meant to prevent fraud and assure that the producer has adhered to a clear set of rules.

Without the certification, anything labelled simply "organic" means you are relying on the word of whoever is calling it that. No one has inspected the farm or production facility, and the food producer hasn't necessarily followed all the regulations established by a certifying body. Different jurisdictions have different certifying bodies, and each body may have slightly different definitions as to exactly what they consider organic. For Vancouver Island and the Gulf Islands, crops, livestock, and processing are accredited by the Islands Organic Producers Association (IOPA). Farmers and food producers who declare that their products are certified organic should be able to produce the paperwork that proves it. If a producer claims that what he or she is selling is organic, or organically grown or produced, that could mean almost anything unless they have the certification to back it up. Transitional organic means that a product is partway through the process of becoming certified organic, which takes three years.

■ **Biodynamic:** Proponents of biodynamic farms and products believe this method of food production is superior to certified organic (or some would say "beyond organic") because it pays more attention to soil, considering it to be one of the living organisms on a farm that must be nurtured and cared for along with the plants and animals. The method emphasizes the use of fermented compost and manures, planting and sowing crops according to the phases of the moon, and land use integration on the farm consisting of crop management, raising livestock, and the overall care of the land. Certification of biodynamic farms is handled in Canada by the Demeter Association.

■ **Free-run, free-range:** Neither of these terms guarantees the product is healthier for you, the animals involved, or the environment. You see these claims most often on egg cartons and sometimes on meat and poultry packaging. Sustainable-food proponents look for free-run or free-range labels, since many of the eggs we eat are still produced by battery hens in small cages. Up to seven birds are crammed into each fifty-by-sixty-centimetre cage. The cages are just thirty-five centimetres tall and are stacked two to eight cages high—as many as four hundred thousand birds can be kept in one dimly lit barn. The birds suffer from feather loss and weakened bone structure and have their beaks removed to help prevent pecking injuries and cannibalism. The overall environment is also at risk because of the amount of manure and ammonia gas produced by these chickens living in such a concentrated space. Free-run means the animal is not living in a cage, but this is not a measurable standard, and the animal may still live in a crowded barn. Free-range means they have access to outdoors, but again, this is not a measurable standard. Free-range does not equal organic. In BC, certified organic eggs have another layer of scrutiny which includes regulations surrounding the birds' diet, range conditions, health care, and transportation. Why should you bother sourcing eggs from a reliable source? First, improved animal welfare, and second, eggs from chickens that are certified organic and free-range are less likely to contain dangerous bacteria such as salmonella, and they are much more nutritious than commercially produced eggs.

■ **Grain-fed, grain-finished, grass-fed, grass-finished, pasture-raised:** Most of these terms apply to beef and other protein sources like chicken, pork, and lamb. Grain is often fed to cows raised for beef; it fattens them quickly and develops the "marbling" of fat in choicer cuts. Some people like that marbling and the taste of the fat, but it comes at a price, since many cows spend at least forty-five days in Concentrated Animal Feeding Operations (CAFOs). The animals are crowded into vegetation-less pens (in the case of cattle, a large CAFO is at least one thousand animals) and fed unnatural diets until they are sent to slaughter to produce the largest amount of animal protein at the least cost to farmers. Unfortunately, this method also increases the risk of spreading dangerous E. coli bacteria and creates waste disposal problems, not to mention a huge amount of methane gas from the belching cows, whose stomachs are not designed to process grain.

Finishing an animal means selecting its diet for the 90 to 120 days before slaughter. Grain-finished means the animals may have been raised on pasture but fattened before slaughter on grain, although not necessarily in a CAFO. You may also see "grain-supplemented" on a label for beef, which may mean the grain fed to the cattle was in small amounts so that the animal wasn't sickened by it. Grass-fed and pasture-raised mean the animals spend their lives in pastures, eating grasses. Grass-finished means the animals ate only grasses and hay leading up to slaughter. This is another case in which it benefits you to do some research and ask questions of the butcher or farmer from whom you are buying your beef. To me, grass-fed beef has a much "beefier" flavour and the side benefit of having higher levels of omega-3 fatty acids and more vitamin E, beta carotene, and vitamin C than CAFO beef. Grass-fed beef and lamb also have less saturated fat, cholesterol, and calories.

Pasture-raised chickens are kept outside in uncrowded bottomless cages that are moved down the pasture daily. The chickens eat the grass and bugs and leave behind their rich droppings to fertilize the pasture as it regrows in time for the next cycle of chickens.

When you are trying to live a more sustainable lifestyle, cost is also a factor. Certified organic, sustainable, and small-scale products are quite often more expensive than their mass-produced counterparts. Some of your eating lifestyle will depend on your economic situation. I've tried to learn how to do more with less. Because the grass-fed beef I buy is so flavourful, I'm satisfied with eating half the amount I used to. Some people choose to buy certified organic fruits and vegetables to replace the "Dirty Dozen," products deemed to have the highest amounts of pesticide residues by the Environmental Working Group. Apples, strawberries, and celery are among the Dirty Dozen. The price differential is dropping, however; and it's great to see certified organic produce sections in grocery stores growing because of the demand—on any given day you may find a certified organic product that costs less than its conventional counterpart. I'm thankful my mom taught me how to be a thrifty shopper, so I pick and choose where to spend my food budget in the most sustainable fashion for me.

The reality is there is no one answer, and it may seem like hard work to make the right choices for you and your family. But look at it this way: part of the homework is getting out and meeting new people like the farmers who grow great ingredients and the artisans who make great products such as cheese, preserves, and cured meats. Try these products cooked for you in local restaurants and from food carts, and then buy them at farmers' markets and cook them at home for you and your family. As we move toward a more sustainable food-producing environment, you will meet more and more people who are just as committed to fresh local flavours and healthy foods as you are. And that's not such a bad bit of homework after all.

Categories

BAKERIES

When I was a kid, my mom would go to a variety of supermarkets on Thursday mornings (the sale flyers came in the paper on Wednesday), and in each store she would cruise by the bakery section and pick out whatever bread or buns were in the "reduced for quick sale" bin. We all ate it at home, as toast, in sandwiches, or eventually as breadcrumbs. I guess price overruled quality of the bread. While living in Terrace, BC, I came to treasure sprouted-wheat bread made with care at Fairhaven Farm near Kitwanga, about an hour's drive from Terrace. Eventually I learned how to make my own bread, which I still do from time to time; however, with excellent bakeries to choose from in Victoria, there really isn't much incentive, since they all do a better job on bread than I do. I've subjected most of the bakeries to my "croissant test" as well. For me, a perfect croissant is very flaky and crisp on the outside, with lots of moist layers of buttery goodness on the inside. Bread and baked goods are very subjective topics for most serious eaters; you may not agree with all my choices here, and chances are I've definitely left a few of the best ones out of this edition, so please let me know where they are and why I should visit them in the near future!

BEVERAGES AND SPECIALTY LIQUIDS

While I am trying to give everyone reading this book a good overall sense of this region's artisan products, wine, beer, and spirits producers have been well covered in other books by other experts in the field. But I couldn't resist adding a few of my favourite beverages to this edition. Some of the products you'll read about here contain alcohol, others do not, and some of them are liquids that you don't really drink, as in the case of the Venturi-Schulze vinegar and verjus. The good news is that, for people who are interested in tasting (or making) specialty spirits, the provincial government has made changes to some of the archaic laws that have been in place for decades. Mind you, the sole purpose of some regulations still in effect as I write this seems to be to discourage artisans from actually being able to make money in the alcohol end of the business.

BUTCHERS, CHARCUTIERS, AND SALUMISTS

Everyone knows what to find at a butcher shop and what butchers do. They take whole animals and cut them into more manageable pieces for the home cook: steaks, chops, chicken breasts, and so on. But you may be less familiar with the somewhat strange sounding *charcuterie* and *salumi*. Charcuterie is a French term (*char* for "sear" and *cuite* for "cooked") for meats (traditionally pork) that have been cooked, cured, or preserved in some way; charcuterie could be something like a chicken pot pie, a fresh sausage, or a complex terrine of *foie gras* stuffed with truffles and baked in a rich pastry. A shop selling these products is also called a charcuterie, while the person performing this art is a charcutier. *Salumi* is an Italian term for cured meat, so a salumist is a person who makes salumi. Salumi includes prosciutto, salami, and pancetta as well as cured sausages, which are infinite in their variations. The best news is that we have a mix of traditionalists and newcomers to the art in this region, making products that, in some instances, mirror their roots in Europe and, in others, add regional twists. Don't be afraid to try things like blood sausage or *guanciale* (cured pork jowl); otherwise, you'll be missing out on new flavours and textures. Butchers, charcutiers, and salumists are "in" professions these days. We lost many small, privately owned firms as the general population started shopping in supermarkets, where most of the butchery is done in a centrally located distribution facility. That trend is reversing as more people demand to know where their meat comes from and ask for more local products. Some of the shops in these sections not only create products for sale in their stores but also prepare goods for other shops and restaurants.

CHOCOLATE

There are many fine chocolate makers on Vancouver Island and the Gulf Islands. Of course, chocolate is not a local ingredient, but more and more of our chocolatiers are starting to work with fair-trade cocoa, which guarantees decent working conditions and wages for the producers. You know there are two types of people in the world—cheese people and chocolate people. I am in the camp of the chocolate people. I could give up eating cheese, but never chocolate. Dark chocolate is my favourite, but I don't mind savouring well-made milk chocolate from time to time.

COFFEE ROASTERS AND TEA BLENDERS

As I sit at my computer writing this, I am sipping from a heady mixture of black Assam tea, cardamom, and vanilla bean, designed to match my Chinese zodiac sign by a tea blender near Duncan. That tea blender and one other have been going through the painstaking process of planting and tending tea plants in favourable climate zones here so we can have a taste of homegrown tea leaves. Tea is my choice in the afternoon and evening, but I must start my day with coffee, and once again we are spoiled with choices. While coffee shops are ubiquitous, the people who own many of the smaller shops roast their own beans, creating signature blends according to their own philosophy of roasting. This category is highly subjective—stating which shop does the best job of roasting coffee beans or has the best blend of tea is to invite fierce debate. Everyone has their own preferences in what they want in a cup of coffee or tea. The companies listed here are those that I have tried personally and like, based on at least one of the following criteria: the quality and flavour of their products, and the service, ambience, and atmosphere of the retail outlets run by the owners. As with beer and wine, we are enjoying a renaissance of creativity in this part of the province with these products. It's easy and cheap to buy your hot or cold beverages in supermarkets, gas stations, and vending machines, but if you venture off the beaten track, your reward is unique flavour crafted in small batches by dedicated entrepreneurs.

COOKING GEAR AND KITCHEN SHOPS

Anyone who has ever visited my kitchen knows that I like good kitchen equipment: high-quality pots and pans, knives, and gadgets. I have strict guidelines when it comes to gadgets. They really must work, and they really have to be useful. You'd be surprised how many gadgets you can buy that don't really make your life all that much easier or don't stand up at all to regular use. The shops you'll find here have all the "good stuff" you need for your own kitchen as well as great gift ideas for the other chefs and cooks in your life.

DAIRY - CHEESE, ICE CREAM, GELATO, YOGURT

British Columbia's dairy industry is in its infancy compared with the Old World, or even the province of Quebec, where cheese making has been going on for centuries. While there isn't the age-old tradition of milking cows and transforming their milk into cheese and other products here, we are catching up quickly, especially with a growing list of artisans on Vancouver Island and the Gulf Islands. Milk production is quite a high-tech operation these days. I've visited farms where cows wear microchips to identify them as they enter the milking parlour and pedometers to monitor the number of steps they take each day. Too many or too few from a cow's average can alert the farmer to a possible illness or agitation. Computers monitor the daily production levels from each cow, and bovine nutritionists create specialized diets to optimize production. It's a far cry from the days of milking by hand into buckets and shipping the milk in metal cans.

This thriving industry provides a local source of milk for drinking and has also spawned artisan production of high-quality cheeses and yogurts, made not just of cow's milk but of sheep's and goat's milk as well. Water buffalo herds are being milked as well, and this milk turns up in cheese, yogurt, and ice cream. Many of our cow's-milk producers belong to the Island Farms co-operative, which was started on Vancouver Island in 1944 but is now owned by Agropur, Canada's largest dairy co-operative. Co-op members own most of the quota, as it's called, across Canada, in accordance with regulations set by provincial milk marketing boards. Luckily, our federal government has never approved the use of growth hormones in dairy cows, as they can be quite detrimental to the long-term health of the cow.

However, some cheeses produced here may have milk ingredients produced outside of Canada in other jurisdictions that do allow growth hormones, such as some of the American states. When you support small makers of artisan dairy products, who use only local milk in their creations, read the labels on those products. You will never see "modified milk products" listed as an ingredient. Modified milk products from the United States, such as skim milk powder, casein, and whey protein concentrates, are allowed in Canadian food products such as cheese with no labelling of their origin. If you believe in better animal welfare as part of a sustainable lifestyle, you will avoid products that may have been produced with milk from cows injected with bovine growth hormone, or rBST. While containers of fresh Canadian milk are never supposed to be produced with rBST, avoid milk products such as cheese and yogurt that list "modified milk products" or "modified milk ingredients" on their labels.

FARMS AND FARMERS

The farms included in this book welcome visitors or have farm-gate or farmers'-market sales. I've always felt that it's important to get to know the farmers in your area. They have their fingers on the pulse of what's happening with the weather and growing seasons and often provide advice on what I should be doing or even not doing in my own garden. Without exception, they are hard workers and usually spend seven days a week during the growing season labouring to provide you with top-quality products. Don't be surprised if you see the names of these farms popping up frequently on restaurant menus around the region, for chefs know a good thing when they taste it, and the direct farm-to-fork movement has been gaining momentum over the past few years. For a full, updated list of farms, you can visit islandfarmfresh.com.

FOOD PRODUCTS

The Food Products section in each region is full of foods that have been manufactured or processed in some way. I would prefer to call them goodies, for lack of a better word. They will add to your enjoyment of food or drink. Many of them are available in the specialty shops listed in the book, but that availability will constantly change and grow, so it's best to check with the company to find out exactly where you can find its creations. In some cases, they may only be found at a farmers' market, but that gives you the chance to get out and meet the people involved in the companies.

When you talk to them, you may start to get a sense of all the hard work they must do. Many of these foodstuffs started as home-kitchen ventures, with daily or weekly piles of pots and pans and counters to clean up, jars to sterilize, or bags to fill and label. Many hours go into creating the names, logos, packaging containers, and labels. Don't forget social media—they need to build a website or blog, get on the various social media platforms, and make sure all the accounts are updated! Not to mention the financial accounts, invoices, receipts, taxes. Once their baby becomes more popular, they might have to create or rent a commercial kitchen, hire employees, and so on. It all becomes a bit daunting, especially when they may have started off on their own or as a couple; then their world changes, for the good, one hopes. It means all they do is think about their creation, the next flavour, the next sale. Somehow, they persevere, and a lot of the devotion comes down to the smile they get from a repeat customer, or a story of a new way their food was enjoyed. All of us eaters are part of the process—these people need our constant support, so get out there and get some goodies!

SEAFOOD, FRESH AND PROCESSED, FISHMONGERS, AND DIRECT FISH SALES

If one were asked to define West Coast cuisine, no doubt fish and shellfish would make their way into the resulting description. It's no wonder—we have some of the finest seafood available anywhere in the world. Entire cookbooks have been written about our Pacific salmon and Dungeness crab. Oh, the crab! I had never bought and cooked a live Dungeness crab until I ended up in the parking lot of a nondescript hotel in Prince Rupert in the mid-1980s. In the back of his beat-up pickup truck, a crabber had a large tote bin full of just-landed crabs. "Five bucks," he said and handed me a plastic bag that seemed alive with activity from any number of points along the bottom seam. After a brief struggle to avoid getting my fingers pinched, I popped the crab into a pot of salty, boiling water. About half an hour later I was surrounded by empty shell, my fingers sticky from crab juices and melted butter. Since I learned how it worked,

Dungeness crab has been part of my diet for over twenty-five years. Salmon? I've had the distinct pleasure (and exhaustion) of landing a few large chinook fighters, later eaten as boneless fillets and carefully cured lox. I've devoured countless chunks of sockeye in sashimi and was educated in the mild yet underrated flavour of a pink salmon that had been treated with kid gloves by a sustainable-minded fisherman who barbecued it right on the deck of his boat. We also can enjoy the most delicate flaky halibut, succulent sablefish, and terrific albacore tuna.

Shellfish are the best in the world here. Tiny Kusshi oysters slurped raw from the shell, or giant beach oysters, breaded and fried; Manila or savoury clams for my *linguine con vongole*; the biggest and juiciest mussels. My favourite small crustaceans are spot prawns, but sidestripe and humpback (also known as king) shrimp can be even more delicious. I even like some of the lesser-known delights, like geoduck, gooseneck barnacles, oolichan, and sea urchin. The best mussels that make an appearance on a regular basis in retail outlets are from Salt Spring Island. Unfortunately, my favourite BC Honey Mussels are hard to come by, even though they are farmed in the northern Gulf Islands. Some of our finest seafood gets sent to Vancouver and beyond immediately, before we ever get a chance to enjoy it. Luckily, the number of fishers who will sell their product directly to the consumer is on the rise. Inside the book you'll find listings for individual boats or co-ops of fishers getting together to offer their products.

Slowly, I'm visiting more seafood shops. They are one of those specialty shops that fell by the wayside when we started going to supermarkets, and because we don't eat as much fish as we should, perhaps, the resurgence in this kind of shop has lagged behind butcher shops, for example. Some supermarkets that have dedicated space to fresh seafood and live tanks with crabs, clams, and mussels have woefully undereducated staff when it comes to providing information consumers want to know: whether the seafood is farmed or wild, where it was caught, when it was caught, and how to cook it. Look for the Ocean Wise logo or those of other sustainable seafood programs on restaurant menus and supermarket and fish-shop counters. That way, you can be sure that the products you are buying are from sustainable sources.

Some of your best bets for finding a high-quality supply of West Coast seafood may be on the docks or at your local farmers' market. Visiting a port where fishers bring in their catch is definitely fun—although you'll have to do some work to figure out a fisher's schedule (always subject to change) and what they might have available. Always ask to see the catch before you buy and ask when it was caught. If a boat has been out for many days, or even a week, you may be better off buying a fish that was frozen soon after it was caught instead of a fresh fish. More and more fishers are also showing up at farmers' markets with frozen or canned products. It's a good opportunity to chat and ask about the sustainable-fishing techniques now practised by many smaller fishers. You could also investigate getting a year-round supply of seafood through a community-supported fishery. These are like community-supported agriculture programs, but instead of paying a farmer upfront for a share in the upcoming crops, you pay a fisher upfront for a share of whatever they catch in the coming season.

SPECIALTY SHOPS AND SPECIALTY GROCERS

I am drawn to specialty food shops in our region like a fly to honey. The great thing is that more shop owners are putting their faith in local food and beverage producers to help stock their shelves and giving them a chance to get known. When an artisan decides to sell to a retailer, it is a major decision that usually requires a greater capital expense, perhaps a profit-sharing arrangement with a distributor, and a much more important commitment to providing what they make on a regular basis—sometimes on a moment's notice. I am very thankful that there are a growing number of shops here that make it easier for island artisans to promote and sell their products. On the other hand, I admit that I am not an ideological everything-I-eat-must-be-local kind of guy. I enjoy eating foods that we can't produce here or are a specialty of a different country, and there's lots of those mentioned in this book, too. Please read on and enjoy!

Comox Valley

Black Creek
Campbell River
Courtenay
Cumberland
Royston

1

frutas
espax
DESAFIO
DESAFIO

COMOX VALLEY

I have a soft spot for the Comox Valley. In this book, the listings cover the space from Campbell River down to Royston and Cumberland. For most of the years I've lived on Vancouver Island, I've spent some time every summer attending the amazing Vancouver Island Music Festival or the exciting BC Shellfish Festival, where I've presented cooking classes, emceed culinary competitions, and judged oyster shucking contests (not for the faint of heart). The Comox Valley Farmers' Market is truly a market for farmers and food artisans, and I've spent many happy Saturday mornings there filling my shopping bags with top quality fresh produce, baked goods, and even bedding plants to take home to my raised-bed gardens in Victoria. I think the restaurants in the Comox Valley were the first outside of Victoria to really embrace the farm-to-table movement as I discovered during my first visits there. Pioneer chefs Ronald St. Pierre at Locals Restaurant really went out of his way to encourage local farmers, but he always demanded top quality and, in that way, encouraged them to be better. I remember going into Locals at its first location and seeing the portraits of the farmer suppliers hanging on the wall and a whole rack of business cards of those farmers. After fifteen years at Locals, Chef St. Pierre and his amazing front-of-house wife Tricia decided to retire in 2023, but the new team in place is as dedicated to maintaining the farmer–chef connection as the original owners were.

Along with the farms, there are many distilleries and wineries to visit, and if winter sports are your thing, the valley is home to the top ski resort on Vancouver Island, Mount Washington. Canadian Forces Base Comox is the major employer in the area, and many of the people who work there have travelled overseas as part of their rotation in the CFB, and I was once told they bring a certain sophistication in food and drink back from their travels, so it's just a little easier for restaurants to expand and modernize their menus to embrace that diversity of palates.

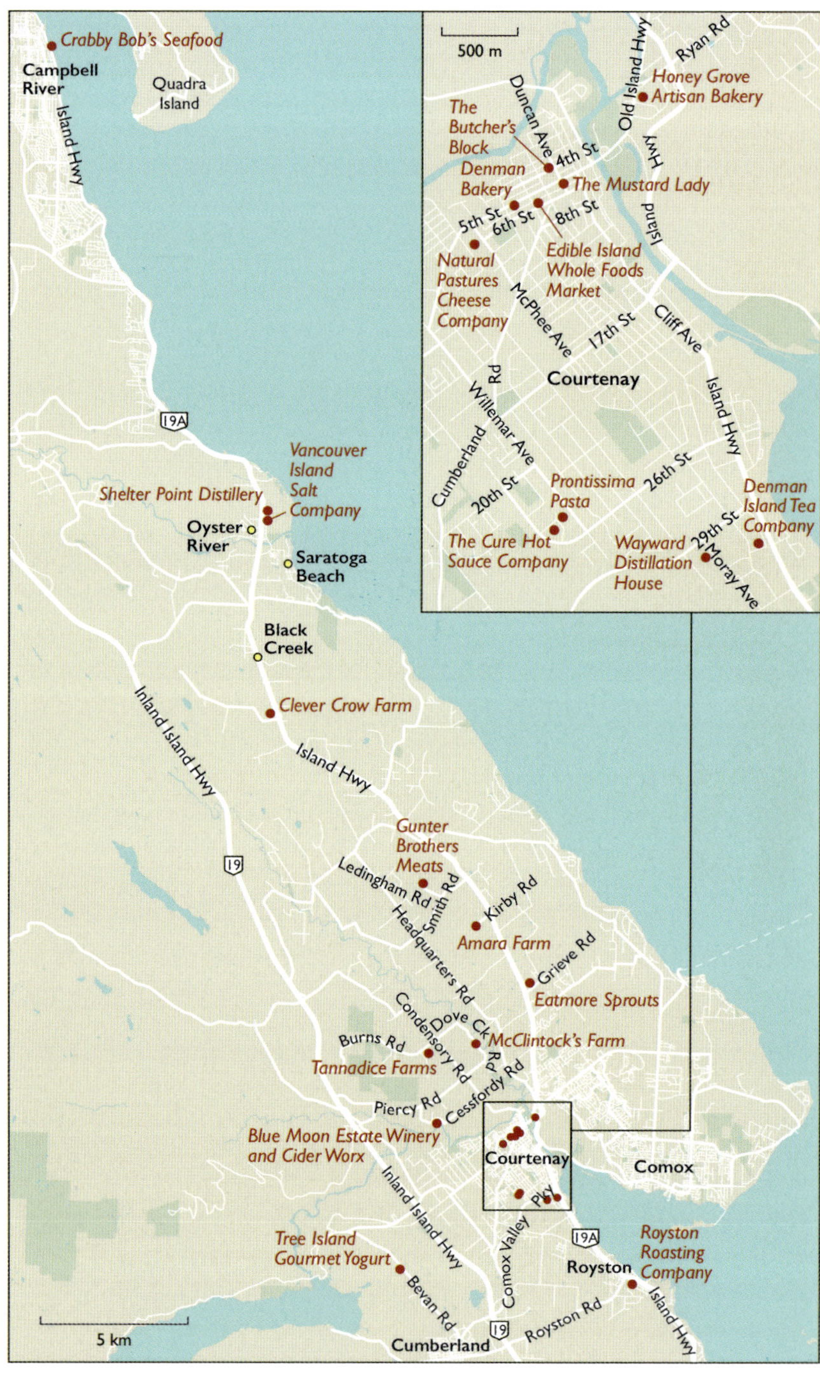

Crabby Bob's Seafood
Campbell River
Quadra Island
Island Hwy
19A
Vancouver Island Salt Company
Shelter Point Distillery
Oyster River
Saratoga Beach
Black Creek
Clever Crow Farm
Inland Island Hwy
Island Hwy
Gunter Brothers Meats
19
Ledingham Rd
Smith Rd
Kirby Rd
Amara Farm
Headquarters Rd
Grieve Rd
Eatmore Sprouts
Condensory Rd
Dove Ck Rd
McClintock's Farm
Burns Rd
Tannadice Farms
Cessford Rd
Piercy Rd
Blue Moon Estate Winery and Cider Worx
Courtenay
Comox
Pky
Inland Island Hwy
Comox Valley
19A
Royston
Royston Roasting Company
Tree Island Gourmet Yogurt
Bevan Rd
5 km
Cumberland
19
Royston Rd
Island Hwy
500 m
Ryan Rd
Old Island Hwy
Duncan Ave
Honey Grove Artisan Bakery
The Butcher's Block
4th St
Hwy
Denman Bakery
The Mustard Lady
5th St
6th St
8th St
Island
Natural Pastures Cheese Company
Edible Island Whole Foods Market
McPhee Ave
17th St
Cliff Ave
Rd
Courtenay
Willemar Ave
Cumberland
Island Hwy
20th St
Prontissima Pasta
26th St
Denman Island Tea Company
The Cure Hot Sauce Company
Wayward Distillation House
29th St
Moray Ave

FOOD ARTISANS OF COMOX VALLEY

Denman Bakery, a.k.a Vassili's Bread Shop

556–5th Street, Courtenay | 250-871-0880 | FB: Vassili's Bread Shop

Bill and Erica Marler.

The Denman Bakery used to be on Denman Island. But while Bill Marler had owned the bakery for over a decade, he had been living for a while in Courtenay. Ferrying back and forth every day just didn't make sense, so when a space well-suited for a bakery became available just a short walk down the street from his house, deciding to move the business to Courtenay was easy. More than twenty-five years later, he still makes sure Denman Islanders get frequent deliveries. Bill's wife Erica told me the business really flourished during the Covid-19 pandemic when people decided to buy local. She even started working there full-time. This bakery has built up a loyal following over the years and serves individuals and wholesale accounts with high-quality sandwich breads and some specialties including the "take and bake" pizza. You phone in your order. They build it for you from scratch, on its own baking sheet. You pick it up, you put it in the oven, and you never ever have cold pizza. Vegans get a dairy-free topping at no extra charge. Long-time favourites are the granola bars called triangles, and there's a growing roster of flavours for the cinnamon buns. You may hear people talking about this bakery by two different names. Bill had visited Greece often enough to earn a nickname there—Vassili. So the sign outside on Fifth Street reads "Denman Bakery presents Vassili's Bread Shop."

Honey Grove Artisan Bakery

Unit B 320 Old Island Highway, Courtenay | 250-898-3304
honeygrovebakery.ca | IG: honeygrovebakery

If there is one rule I've learned over the years I've spent attending farmers' markets it's to look for the long line-ups. Invariably the line-up will reveal something worth waiting for. That was the case when I first saw the line-up for Honey Grove Artisan Bakery at the Comox Valley Farmers' Market. The line-up was worth it. The bread I bought was excellent and so were the pastries. Honey Grove specializes in slow fermented, small batch sourdough bread and pastries made from certified organic Canadian flour. It was the bread that first attracted current bakery owners Lili Yacub and Bo Waite to Mark Sims's bread, which was first baked on a wood-fired oven at his farm in Merville. When he moved production into Courtenay, it happened to be right across from the office where Bo worked as medical assistant. An avid home bread maker, she liked this bread so much she took on a part-time job with Mark Sims. It was the same for Lili Yacub. Lili had returned from living in France and couldn't believe she could buy bread in the Comox Valley that was better than anything she had there. She started working at the bakery, too, but on opposite shifts from Bo, so they had only met each other once before when Mark Sims announced he was moving out of the country and wanted out of the bakery. Neither Bo nor Lili knew much about running a bakery, but they couldn't stand the idea of that wonderful bread coming to an end. They wanted to keep making what

Lily Yacub and Bo Waite.

» Honey Grove Artisan Bakery

they love. They came to an agreement to buy the business from Mark, and he agreed to finance them so they could get started. The rest, as they say, is history. Lili says their partnership sounds like an arranged marriage while Bo says it has been an incredibly steep learning curve. They took over in 2019, just before the pandemic, managed to survive that, and then a year-long battle for Lili with cancer, but the bakery continues to thrive. The biggest news for them in 2024 was the purchase of a new-to-them pastry oven which allowed them to be much more efficient in their baking, especially with the other big news being the opening of an official storefront for Honey Grove much closer to downtown than their production facility. There will be more parking . . . and maybe shorter line-ups.

Blue Moon Estate Winery and Cider Worx (Raven's Moon Craft Cider)

4905 Darcy Road, Courtenay | 250-338-9765 | ravensmooncraftcider.ca
FB: Raven's Moon Craft Cider & Blue Moon Farm

Father and son team George and Quinn Ehrler.

What's in a name? A lot. It all starts with the farm. George Ehrler and Marla Limousin grow blueberries, blackberries, apples, and strawberries on Blue Moon Farm, where the fruits from the farm and other Vancouver Island and BC sources are turned into fruit wines and ciders at the Blue Moon Estate Winery and Cider Worx. They also operate Raven's Moon Craft Cider. Fruit wines sometimes get a deservedly bad rap. They can be horrible, especially in the hands of amateurs like your Uncle Louie. But the quality of fruit wines and ciders and liqueurs from Vancouver Island has been improving to award-winning levels. This is very apparent here. Engineer-by-trade George decided to get a little bit more serious with the winemaking hobby he had pursued for years. So he built a winery attached

» Blue Moon Estate Winery and Cider Worx

to the farm-gate store and eventually added cider to his creations. One specialty not to miss is Lunacy, a dessert wine made from organic blueberries and wild blackberries which is then blended and aged in oak barrels. George likes to keep the production small so he can meet potential customers coming in the door. "Our biggest hurdle is getting over the memories people have of the fruit wine their elders used to make down in the basement, and how they didn't really enjoy it. But we have people coming in here now and tasting and saying how it's different than what they remember, and they like it."

Shelter Point Distillery

4692 Regent Road, Campbell River | 778-420-2200
shelterpoint.ca | IG: shelterpoint

I first visited the Shelter Point Distillery back in 2013, when the distillers were still a year away from bottling their first Canadian whiskey. I was lucky enough to taste a sample of the soon-to-be-whiskey direct from one of the oak barrels, and I knew even then it was going to be good. I toured Shelter Point again ten years later and . . . good news. The distillery is still an amazing building just a few metres from the ocean featuring beautiful woodwork, stonework, and the truly magnificent copper stills imported from Scotland. A lot of the barley used in making Shelter Point whiskey is grown on the farmland surrounding the distillery, and the water comes from an aquifer on the property. The ocean even has a role when it comes to aging the whiskey. A warehouse close to the ocean has its doors thrown open to the salty breezes wafting through the barrels to add a salty nuance, and Shelter Point's Smoke Point is a single malt further augmented by aging in barrels that, when empty, were smoked under fires built from driftwood found on the shoreline of the property. All the attention to detail over the years has resulted in a flight of fine whiskies, including a couple of double-gold winners at the World Spirits Competition. Tastings and tours of the distillery are available.

Chris Read of Shelter Point Distillery in the beachside whiskey-aging warehouse.

Wayward Distillation House

2931 Moray Avenue, Courtenay | 250-871-0424
waywarddistillery.com | IG: waywarddistillery

I had known for a long time that mead was a very ancient beverage, a kind of wine made from honey. What I didn't know is that you could also take honey and turn it into spirits. That's what Dave Brimacombe and Laura Carbonell do at the Wayward Distillation House in Courtenay. My first experience with their products was a tasting of their Krupnik, a full forty percent alcohol by volume Polish-style spiced honey liqueur. It is exquisite, smooth, and full of flavour from the addition of cinnamon, nutmeg, vanilla, and citrus peel. My wife says it tastes "like Christmas," and I can't disagree—although you don't have to restrict the enjoyment of it to the holiday season, it's fine for sipping year-round and is one of Wayward's top sellers. So . . . a honey liqueur made from honey makes sense, but Wayward also turns out gins, rum, and vodka. The honey comes from an apiary in BC's Peace River Region that has grown the number of hives they have with the growth of Wayward. The bees' first task is being taken around to different farms to help in pollinating crops. When the hives come back to home base they rest on clover, and the honey resulting from those blossoms is sent to Wayward. Fermenting honey can sometimes be tricky, and sometimes Wayward needs to give its bees and beekeepers a break, so they've started producing some spirit from grains as well, like their craft vodka. The tasting room at Wayward Distillation House puts you close to the fermenting process so you can learn about that when you visit, but they also have some demonstration hives outside so you can learn about bees and honey at the same time. Wayward Distillery donates one percent of spirit sales to the protection and promotion of bees and pollinators via Pollinator Partnership Canada.

o **Laura Carbonell, Distiller.**

The Butcher's Block

319–4th Street Courtenay | 250-338-1412
thebutchersblock.ca | FB: The Butcher's Block

Greg and Colby Wilson.

Owner Greg Wilson of the Butcher's Block in downtown Courtenay has been cutting meat and preparing and feeding people for over three decades now. After working in restaurants on the mainland, he came back to his roots on Vancouver Island to help the original owner of the business open a restaurant. But soon he learned how to "cut" as they say in the butcher's trade, and a year later, bought the business. Greg says most people come to the shop for service, quality, and pricing. And the sausages. Greg has full-time employees solely dedicated to making sausages with recipes they have been tweaking for over thirty years. The sausages are definitely tasty, and people line up at lunchtime to grab sandwiches made with not only the meats from the shop but other local condiments they also sell there. Greg's son has decided to join his father in the business, and that's good news as it ensures a much-beloved business will continue to thrive while Greg takes some well-deserved rest!

Gunter Brothers Meats

6200 Ledingham Road, Courtenay | 250-334-2960
gunterbros.com | IG: gunter.bros

Gunter Brothers Meats has been a family-owned and -operated business in the Comox Valley since 1932. While brothers Dennis and Harry Gunter took over from their father in 1987, they can trace their craft back to their grandfather, who founded the company as an on-farm facility when he moved here from England. He learned his trade from his own grandfather, so we are talking five generations. The current processing plant and retail store sits just north of Courtenay, a collection of unassuming green metal-clad buildings. I toured the processing plant and was impressed with its collection of modern processing equipment and attention to cleanliness and detail. Once you step inside the retail shop, though, the unmistakable aroma of smoked meat asserts itself, and you know you are in a place that takes its art seriously. You'll find a wide selection of fresh, frozen, and cured products along with a smattering of other common deli products like mustards and colourful cans of spices. Where this company really shines is in its service as a slaughterhouse and processor for local livestock farmers. Without this kind of facility, it just wouldn't be possible for them to economically get their products to market.

Harry and Dennis Gunter.

YEAR ROYAL
PUERH

Denman Island Tea Company

13–2998 Kilpatrick Avenue, Courtenay | 250-334-1043
denmantea.ca | IG: denmantea.ca

Brendan Waye is a certified tea sommelier. Yes, there is such a thing, and Brendan has been involved with the tea industry for decades. I first met him many years ago when he was known as "The Tea Guy" in Vancouver but was pleasantly surprised to find out he is now the owner of the Denman Island Tea Company in Courtenay. His main business these days is supplying cafés on Vancouver Island and beyond with carefully curated teas to serve their customers, but he also does a lot of mail order to individuals and operates the storefront on Kilpatrick Avenue. It's called the Denman Island Tea Company because Brendan is stubbornly trying to establish a tea plantation on some of the Mediterranean-type microclimates he found there. It's a tough go. The weather hasn't been co-operating, but his first harvest is expected in 2025. In the meantime, the tea sommelier imports and blends only organic teas from Japan, India, and Africa and is trying to locally source more and more of his herbs used in certain blends such as lavender from a farm in the Cowichan Valley or peppermint from the San Juan Islands.

Brendan Waye, Tea Sommelier.

Royston Roasting Coffee House

3904 Island Highway, Royston | 250-871-8666
rrcocoffee.com | IG: roystonroasting

I admit it: I like shiny, bright objects. That's what drew me to Dyan Spink's table at the Comox Valley Farmers' Market a few years ago. Dyan, the founder of Royston Roasting, was selling coffee beans she had roasted herself, but the photo on her table showed the bright, shiny drum-style roaster with the hand-tooled copper cladding that came all the way from Turkey. The roastery and café, right on the Old Island Highway, now houses that beautiful roaster in the basement, where current owners Jessie and Gavin Drew Taylor preside over the roasting as well as the café offering their coffee products, teas from Hornby Island Tea, and breakfast and lunch selections including sandwiches, sweet treats, and croissants from Honey Grove Artisan Bakery. Many of the coffees offered are fair trade or Rainforest Alliance certified.

Jessie and Gavin Drew Taylor.

Natural Pastures Cheese Company

635 McPhee Avenue, Courtenay | 250-334-4422
naturalpastures.com | IG: naturalpasturescheese

Doug Smith and Paul Sutter in the cheese aging room.

Fine cheese comes from quality milk, and that's the secret to the award-winning cheeses from Natural Pastures. The milk tradition started three generations ago with the Smith family of Beaver Meadow Farms in the Comox Valley. In 2001, Smith brothers Edgar, Phillip, and Doug saw a way to capitalize on the excellent milk they were producing by adding value to it in the form of cheese. Now, in addition to the milk from their own farm, they select milk from other carefully chosen dairy farms in the area and water buffalo milk from two different Vancouver Island farms. Not only must the milk be of excellent quality, but the farms themselves must meet sustainability standards set by Natural Pastures. Head cheese maker Paul Sutter is Swiss born and trained and started making award-winning cheeses for the Smiths as soon as he joined the company in 2002, and as the company expanded, he has taken new, younger cheese makers under his wing. I think part of their success is thinking outside the box a bit, as along with standard brie- and Camembert-style cheeses, they produce some unusual smoked and flavoured cheeses, such as their smoked Dutch-style boerenkaas, and three varieties based on verdelait, a combination of cheddar, Dutch Gouda, and Swiss raclette. My favourite is the Cracked Pepper Verdelait.

Tree Island Gourmet Yogurt

2800 Beck Avenue, Cumberland | 250-334-0608
treeislandyogurt.com | IG: treeislandyogurt

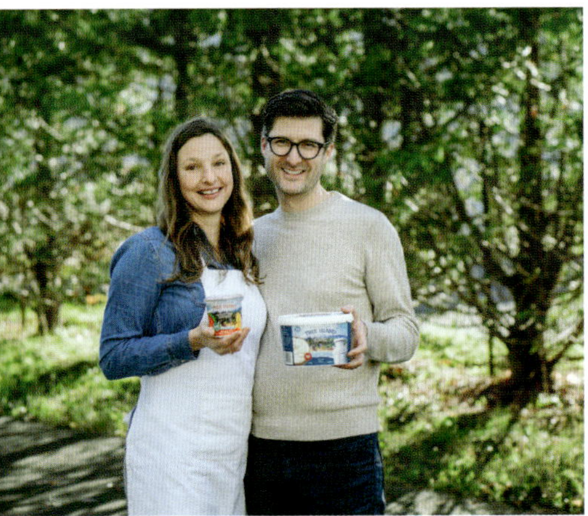

Merissa Myles and Scott DiGuistini.

Scott DiGuistini and Merissa Myles decided to make yogurt part of their lifestyle when they started their family. They had a "yogurt epiphany" on a trip to France, tasting yogurt that they had never tasted before; it was plain and simple and not industrialized like most of our yogurt in Canada. Scott says many Canadian yogurts are made by just two or three companies, with milk from all over Canada, so they thought going local gave them an immediate advantage. Tree Island uses milk from grass-fed cows from carefully selected BC dairy farms, and they use just whole milk; nothing is taken out and nothing added in other than the bacterial cultures necessary for proper fermentation and some seasonal flavours like Pacific Strawberry and Okanagan Peach. They first built a state-of-the-art processing plant in Royston, but outgrew that facility and constructed a new, larger facility in nearby Cumberland. Meanwhile the number of retailers carrying their cream-top and local honey yogurts has increased enormously. With an extra eye to the environment, Tree Island Yogurt packaging now contains fifty percent less plastic. Competition is steep in the yogurt section, and their price is higher than common industrial yogurts, but once you taste it and realize how pure a product it is, you'll be hooked.

Amara Farm

2641 Kirby Road, Courtenay | 250-702-5657
amarafarm.ca | FB: Amara Farm

Arzeena Hamir and Neil Turner.

Arzeena Hamir and Neil Turner named their farm using a combination of their daughter's, first names, but Arzeena also told me Amara means "gift". And Amara Farm is a gift to anyone visiting there or shopping their products at the Comox Valley Farmers Market. The certified organic goodness lasts all year long; the last summer I visited the farm I picked up ten pounds of the plump Amara blueberries, some of which I stashed in the freezer for smoothies and baking right through the winter. Other must-try products they are proud of include garlic, asparagus, and black currants. And coming right along is a hazelnut orchard, which was planted a few years ago and is doing very well.

Island Pastures Beef

Available exclusively at Country Grocers supermarkets on Vancouver Island
FB: Island Pastures Beef

Over twenty years ago, rancher Brad Chappell returned to his home in the Comox Valley to re-establish his ranching roots there. He soon realized that Vancouver Island was a difficult place to produce beef and make the effort worthwhile. He brought together a group of about a dozen beef producers, mostly in the Comox Valley, with the idea of a co-op that would supply retailers with Island-raised, grass-fed, grass-finished beef. The Country Grocer supermarket chain, with eleven locations up and down the island, stepped up in a big way and has been a true supporter of Island Pastures Beef all these years. Chappell told me consumers are willing to pay a bit of a premium for a consistent, high-quality product that also helps promote agricultural sustainability and diversity because of the varied grassland "salads" the ranchers grow to feed their animals.

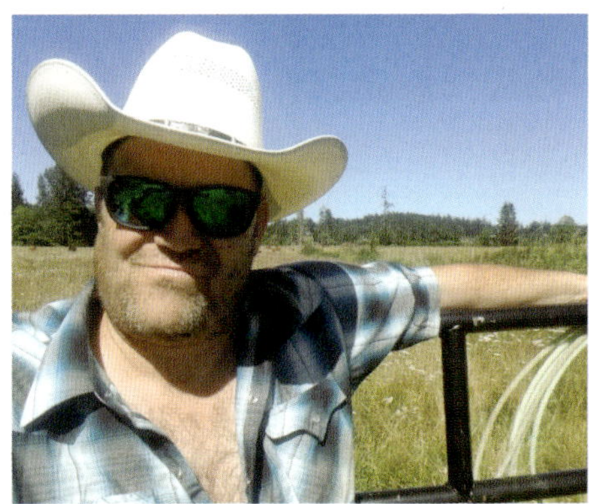

Brad Chappell.

McClintock's Farm

3419 Dove Creek Road, Courtenay | 250-334-4562
mcclintocksfarm.ca | FB: McClintock's Farm

Sandra McClintock

There's a photo of Gerry McClintock in the first edition of this book. I took it at the Comox Valley Farmers' Market simply because it was a nice picture of a farmer unloading dozens of cobs of corn from a fully loaded pickup truck with a handmade sign proclaiming this was a fresh and sweet new crop from McClintock's Farm. Apparently, Gerry heard from quite a few people telling him he was in the book. But I didn't actually meet Gerry and his daughter Sandra until a few years later when on another tour of the Comox Valley. I didn't go there to the farm for the corn, I wanted to see their water buffalo operation. Why? Because I was familiar with the ancestry of some of their herd. When I lived in the Cowichan Valley, I was a frequent visitor to Fairburn Farm, home of Canada's first water buffalo herd. The folks at Fairburn sold fifteen of their heifers to the McClintocks, and in 2012, Sandra started milking them. It's not as easy running a water buffalo herd as it is a herd of dairy cows, but somehow, they've managed to make it

» McClintock's Farm

work. Now the herd is around two hundred strong, and their milk is sent to nearby Natural Pastures Cheese to make a version of the famous Italian product, Mozzarella di Bufala. Natural Pastures also makes other buffalo milk cheeses like bocconcini, feta, and paneer. While those cheeses are Natural Pastures branded, if you go the dairy section of a grocery store on Vancouver Island you just may find McClintock's Water Buffalo yogurt. The milk has a different flavour and creamier texture with more protein and higher percentages of beneficial minerals and vitamins than cow's milk. You'll find the yogurt in grocery stores all around Vancouver Island and the province in general and as far away as Toronto. Parachute Ice Cream in Victoria uses their milk to make some of their ice cream. At the farm you will also find U-Pick blueberries and raspberries in season, the aforementioned corn, water buffalo meat in a variety of cuts, and you will still find Gerry at the Comox Valley Farmers' Market with a full pickup truck when the corn is ready.

Tannadice Farms

3465 Burns Road, Courtenay | 250-338-8239
tannadicefarms.com | FB: Tannadice Farms Ltd

For me, Tannadice Farms is all about healthy, happy pigs. Although Heather and Allen McWilliam also raise black and red Angus cattle and turkeys, it was their pig operation that first attracted my attention when I visited their farm, and it wasn't because of a horrible smell—rather, a *lack* of smell. The barns where the pigs are raised are very well-ventilated, and the pigs have lots of clean sawdust to roll around in. I also didn't hear a lot of squealing or fighting. Happy, clean pigs. This is quite important when it comes to the finished product. Pigs that are stressed because of their living conditions or from being transported long distances to slaughter could result in meat with a pale, unattractive colour, or poor, watery texture. The Tannadice Farms brand is familiar now to shoppers up and down the island, with many grocery stores, meat shops, and farm shops carrying a variety of cuts. One of my favourites includes the country-style cut rib, which I love cooking low and slow on my pellet smoker. For a wider range of products, try buying direct from the farm. You can just drop by, but it's better to make an appointment by calling ahead. Ask if you can see the pigs in their barn: there's nothing like the sight of some placid porcines to make your day.

Allen McWilliam.

Clever Crow Farm

7911 N Island Highway, Black Creek | 250-465-0448
clevercrowfarm.com | IG: clevercrowfarm

Lia and Brian McCormick in their farm store.

Near Courtenay, Lia and Brian McCormick operate Clever Crow Farm. Before they bought their current farm, they were making sea salt from scratch, boiling down ocean water to be left with salt. When they had nailed down their base, they started to get creative with infusing the salt with up to ten different flavours, including citrus, rosemary, and seaweed. But when they added their five-acre farm into the mix, they decided to source their salt instead of making it to save themselves a lot of time. Now many of the herbs and even the chili peppers they grow on the farm are added to the salts, and they grind and blend imported spices into fresh, small batch blends. The farm store on their property is open March through December to sell their own produce as well as products from other island artisans and beyond. Add in occasional cooking classes with guest chefs, and I don't know when they have time to put their feet up for a well-deserved rest!

Eatmore Sprouts

2604 Grieve Road, Courtenay | 250-338-4860
eatmoresprouts.com | IG: eatmoresprouts

Carmen and Glenn Wakeling.

It's easy to dismiss a box of alfalfa sprouts or pea shoots as just another product you pick up at the grocery store until you see how much work goes into making sure the sprouts in the store are as safe, delicious, and nutritious as when they left the place where they were created. After touring the certified organic Eatmore Sprouts facility in Courtenay, I left with a new appreciation for how these delicate, tiny plants are ready for eating within just a few days of being started from seed. Carmen Wakeling clearly displayed a lot of pride in the operation she and her husband, Glenn, have built since they took it over a couple of decades ago. Sprouts can be contaminated with some food-borne illnesses, even when they are unsprouted seeds, so that's where Eatmore's quality control starts, and it continues all the way through to the packaging and shipping of their entire line, including sunflower, garlic, clover, and broccoli sprouts. It's fascinating to see all stages of the sprouts' growing process, through the staged container system Carmen and Glenn have, and even more impressive to see how they compost any waste into beautiful new growing medium for the next cycle of sprouts. You can find Eatmore Sprouts in the Comox Valley, across Vancouver Island and the BC mainland, and as far west as Alberta and Saskatchewan.

The Mustard Lady

510 Duncan Avenue, Courtenay | 250-871-0109
themustardladycv.com | IG: themustardladycv

Stephanie and Brody Abbat-Slater.

The original Mustard Lady, Nancy Farey, started making mustards as a hobby in her Courtenay kitchen back in 2011. Pretty soon she had a lot of fans of her products, so she eventually created a company and then opened a store in downtown Courtenay, complete with a commercial kitchen in 2017. Fast forward to the pandemic. This is where Stephanie and Brody Abbat-Slater come in. Stephanie was involved in the film industry in Toronto, and Brody was a general manager of a restaurant, both of which basically shut down during those first tough months of the pandemic. They decided to move back to Vancouver Island where Brody grew up. There they met the Mustard Lady and really got to know her. Stephanie and Brody had just become parents to a pair of bouncing baby girls, and Nancy watched them grow. The friendship and love of her products continued, so when Nancy wanted to get out of the mustard business, she asked if they wanted to buy the company. They said yes and decided to keep the original name. Since then, they've turned the shop on Duncan Avenue into a colourful, cozy, comfy kind of place and reworked all the labelling and packaging. I met a very enthusiastic Brody at the Cumberland Farmers' Market one Sunday and tasted my way through some of their mustards and pickles. I especially like the candied and pickled jalapenos, and my greatest praise is reserved for the mustard pickles. The sauce surrounding the pickles tastes exactly like what my mom used to make, and I unashamedly admit to drinking the leftover sauce right out of the jar! Yes, it is that good.

Prontissima Pasta

Unit C–2384 Rosewall Crescent, Courtenay | 250-338-3636
IG: prontissimapasta

Prontissima Pasta got its start on a sailboat moored in Venice for the winter. Sarah and Derek Walsh learned to speak Italian and make pasta. To cut a very long story short, they eventually came to Courtenay and created a small shop and storefront to sell fresh pasta. Their former employee, Robin Fitzgerald, bought into the company in 2019 and eventually owned it outright starting in 2022. That's after surviving the pandemic. Robin had a background in catering, and that helped the company survive the pandemic by creating a drive-up window, and many more options beyond lasagna and pasta baked for customers eager to avoid fast food. Robin started doing cannelloni after seeing a corny cartoon somewhere. It involved a farfalle and a penne at a party, looking across the room at a lone pasta shape. "Gee, he's looking cannelloni?" Get it? Cannelloni, kind of lonely? Robin knows it's corny, but somehow it stuck in her head and cannelloni made its debut on the menu. You'll also find soups and curries and even burritos. Desserts are another great Italian feature, cannoli. But the pasta in Prontissima Pasta is still a main feature of the shop, and you will find a great variety of extruded pastas there in various shapes and colours as Robin adds vegetable purees like beet and spinach to liven them up.

Robin Fitzgerald.

The Cure Hot Sauce Company

A1-2351 Rosewall Crescent, Courtenay | 604-353-9430
thecurehotsauce.ca | IG: thecurehotsauceco

Rob Schrier had spent thirty years in the restaurant business . . . he started when he was twelve years old, cooking hot dogs at a drive-in. By 2021, he was done with the industry. It had become toxic to him, and he was burnt out. So, what to do next? For the last twelve years of his career, he'd been a saucier, so he knew how to make sauces. He told me, "I like to sweat when I eat," so making hot sauces was a natural transition. After some trial and error, he was ready to join some other food artisans like Prontissima Pasta at the Tin Town complex in Courtenay, a collection of unique businesses well worth a visit. Rob's space includes a commercial kitchen as well as a storefront and his entire business has been certified green by BC Green Business and "Surf Rider Approved" by BC Ocean Friendly Business. His hot sauces are made from a variety of different peppers, many of them sourced from Comox Valley farms or grown in his own garden. He's discovered that some hot peppers aren't just hot; they can be very flavourful too, and he works hard on drawing out the flavours. Rob says, "a smoked Carolina Reaper is wonderful." That pepper, the hottest in the world according to the Scoville scale, is a key ingredient in one of his most popular products, Reap Tide. Other best sellers include Goblin Green, made with jalapeno and cilantro, and Black Chili Lime. I think my favourite name is the Mangolorian, made with mangos and habanero peppers. Rob and his wife Jaimes toss around the names after Rob has come up with a new sauce, and she designs all the labels, too. Their take on his version of Worcestershire sauce? Worcesterschrier, of course. Hot sauces are a very competitive market, but The Cure's growth has been exponential, and they're carving out a niche with their unique blends.

Rob Schrier at the Cumberland Farmers' Market.

Vancouver Island Salt Company

4600 Regent Road, Campbell River | 250-686-3862
canadianseasalt.com | IG: vanislesalt

Morgan Rogers and Scott Gibson at the waters of Oyster Bay, the source of their sea salt.

This may sound hard to believe, but I once got very excited watching water boil. The charge came from watching our first West Coast artisan sea salt manufacturer, Andrew Shepherd, of the Vancouver Island Salt Company. As I walked up his driveway in Cobble Hill, I took in the aroma of a wood fire and simmering pots of ocean water, and there was Andrew stoking the fire, evaporating the salt water until there was nothing left but beautiful salt crystals. Why salt? As a trained chef, Andrew couldn't see the sense in using imported sea salt in his cooking when we are surrounded by salt water here on Vancouver Island. So he started experimenting, at first boiling down a ten-litre bucket of sea water until he was left with salt crystals. Friends loved it, so he started using large stockpots over open wood fires to make more. Then he used large cauldrons fired with recycled vegetable oil. A few years ago, Shepherd sold his share of the

» Vancouver Island Salt Company

company to his partners Scott and Lee Gibson, and they, along with a third partner in Morgan Rogers, produce the salt in Black Creek, near Campbell River, on a 400-acre farm on the Oyster Bay shoreline. The seawater is harvested at high tide, filtered to remove any impurities, then boiled in tanks to concentrate the brine, then evaporators to create the salt crystals. The line of salts includes fine salt, flaked salt, a couple of smoked salts, and even a salt infused with Kaplansky's Deli mustard. Vancouver Island Salt Co. also partners with four different Canadian chocolate manufacturers, including Sirene of Victoria, to produce bars and caramels using their salt. One of the newest products is nigari, a brine primarily made from magnesium chloride, one of the byproducts of salt making. Nigari is a traditional coagulant used in making tofu, ricotta cheese, and even sauerkraut, kimchi, and bread. Scott told me they try to use every part of the water they draw from the ocean, not just the salt. Including the nigari, desalinated water is produced that can be used on nearby farms, and minerals used for soil enhancement. The saltworks aren't set up for tours, but in the summer the company sets up an Airstream trailer on the beach like a farm-gate shop, and you're free to wander up and down a pristine beach that extends for kilometres.

Crabby Bob's Seafood

705 Island Hwy # 6F, Campbell River | crabbybobs.ca | IG: Crabby Bob's

Abby Morris with a couple of her bestsellers

The Crabby Bob's backstory is sad, but it has a happy ending. Abby Morris, now known as Crabby Abby, was asked to take care of the shop because her father-in-law, Ray Philipow, had fallen ill. Ray had purchased the business from the original Crabby Bob just a year previously, fulfilling a lifelong dream of owning a business like Crabby Bob's. The dream was cut short when he passed away just two weeks after asking Abby to fill in for him. Running the business definitely hadn't been on Abby's bucket list—she had been thinking about going back to school. But she persevered, and after a couple of years of trying to figure everything out she was in it for the long haul. She's been at it for around fifteen years now, and the business has expanded, not only selling fresh and frozen seafood, but providing a lunch service as well with a small patio for you to enjoy your meal right there by the ocean. In addition to classics like seafood chowder and oysters Rockefeller, Crabby Bob's can feed your whole crowd with small to large platters of freshly steamed crab, shellfish, smoked seafood or a classic West Coast Crab Boil, which includes crab, clams, mussels, scallops, oysters, Andouille sausage, and sweet corn on the cob. I am getting pretty darn hungry just thinking about that one!

Edible Island Whole Foods Market

477–6th Street, Courtenay | 250-334-3116
edibleisland.ca | FB: Edible Island Whole Foods Market

Steve Stewart.

I know that in the times I've shopped around Edible Island, I had that feeling like I had stepped a bit into the past, when "whole foods" meant oats and beans in bulk and lots of "good for you" food products on the shelves with an aroma that just kind of emanated "old-fashioned goodness." When current owner and general manager Steve Stewart talks about the beginnings of Edible Island, I completely understand why I feel that way in the shop. Edible Island was started in 1980, when Steve says, "It started as a food co-op, with like-minded people, frustrated with the food industry, and wanting to eat organic fruit, veggies, and grains. They periodically drove a five-ton truck up to the Okanagan, picked up their orders from a variety of (organic) farms, and then drove back to distribute to members." The members eventually started selling any excess they had to the public, and then the retail outlet was born. When Steve is asked what customers like the most about Edible Island? "Transparency. Local. Connection. Trust. We are on a first name basis with many of our customers, we all have similar values. Just like us, they enjoy supporting local. They like being able to pronounce all the ingredients to what they are putting into their bodies. And they like knowing who is selling them their food—and often who is making it!"

SATURDAY SOJOURN

You may notice a trend in my suggested day trips. They all include visits to a farmers' or public market. But this is where a lot of the food culture in a community originates, and the **Comox Valley Farmers' Market** is no exception. The important news is that, if you get an early start, you can have breakfast at the market. I see a diversity and abundance of produce here that not all markets can match, and it's the only place where I've managed to find some Padrón pepper plants for my garden. After the market I recommend a visit (in season) to **Nature's Way Farm** for fresh organic blueberries and strawberries, which is also the home of **Blue Moon Estate Winery** and **Raven's Moon Craft Cider**, open for tastings of George Ehrler's fruit wines and ciders. If you're nice, I'm sure he'll show you where all the winemaking takes place, just behind the wine shop and teaching kitchen. Get some fresh fruit for your upcoming walk on the beach.

From Courtenay, make your way north. First to **Gunter Brothers Meats**. Pick up something for the barbecue (make sure you pack a cooler and some ice packs) or the breakfast box for the next morning, which contains eggs, sausages, bacon, and hash browns. Keep heading north toward Campbell River. Take your fresh fruit with you when you get to the **Vancouver Island Salt Company** at Black Creek. In the summer you can go for a long walk on their private beach, snacking first on fruit, then stocking up on your salt supply at their converted Airstream trailer "salt box". Head north again to **Shelter Point Distillery**. Marvel first at the architecture of the building housing the stills, then do a tasting and marvel at the fine whiskey flavours developed in their casks. The tasting should whet your palate for a late lunch. One final stop north to **Crabby Bob's Seafood**, then, and if the weather's nice, choose from their variety of fresh seafood selections to enjoy on the patio right on the ocean. Life doesn't get much better than that.

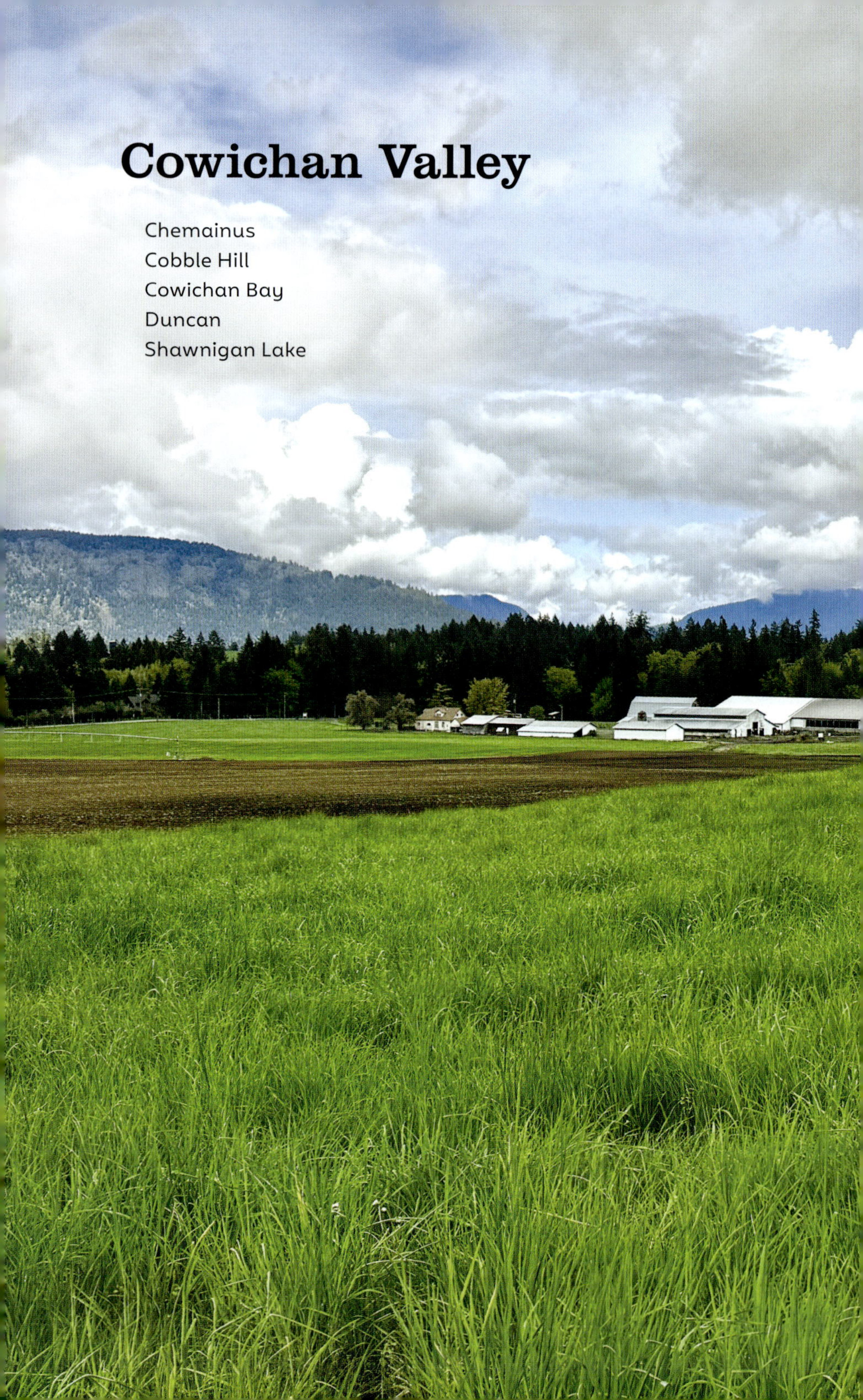

Cowichan Valley

Chemainus
Cobble Hill
Cowichan Bay
Duncan
Shawnigan Lake

2

COWICHAN VALLEY

When I was first considering a move to Vancouver Island in the early 2000s, it was a toss-up between the Saanich Peninsula and the Cowichan Valley. Cowichan won the toss, partly because it was a little cheaper to buy a house there, but mostly because I had already visited a few times and had made new friends, while discovering some of my old acquaintances from Vancouver were already living there. The late, great TV chef and cookbook writer James Barber's move had just preceded my own, and I remember using some of his old moving boxes. And then there was Bill Jones. The chef and restaurant consultant had moved over a few years previously and set up shop at Deerholme Farm, where he still teaches cooking classes, puts on amazing dinners, and teaches people all about foraging and mushroom hunting from his property in Glenora just outside of Duncan. The Cowichan Valley remains a special place for me with its many back roads leading to farms and farmers raising everything from donkeys to geese to pastured chicken. Some of the best dairy farms in the province are there, and you'll find many places to pick up blueberries and strawberries, and you can even visit a tea plantation. Cowichan Bay is a little gem of a town perched right on the ocean, and there are little hamlets tucked here and there on your travels like Cowichan Station, Cobble Hill, and the aforementioned Glenora. Taking the long drive from Cowichan Bay to Genoa Bay reveals some stunning scenery and a great little café at the end of the road with a modern menu featuring local seafood and produce from nearby farms. There are some top-notch wineries to visit like Blue Grouse and Unsworth Vineyards, and right next door to Unsworth is Merridale Cidery and Distillery, where co-owner Janet Docherty has been a tireless leader of promoting the Cowichan Valley tourist industry. There are many places to hike and ride your bike, includ-

ing a great stretch of the Trans Canada Trail that touches right on the edge of Bill Jones's Deerholme Farm, and every so often I have to visit the spectacular Kinsol Trestle, one of the largest and tallest wooden rail trestles in the world. The trains are long gone, but now you can walk or ride your bike or even a horse across the refurbished span.

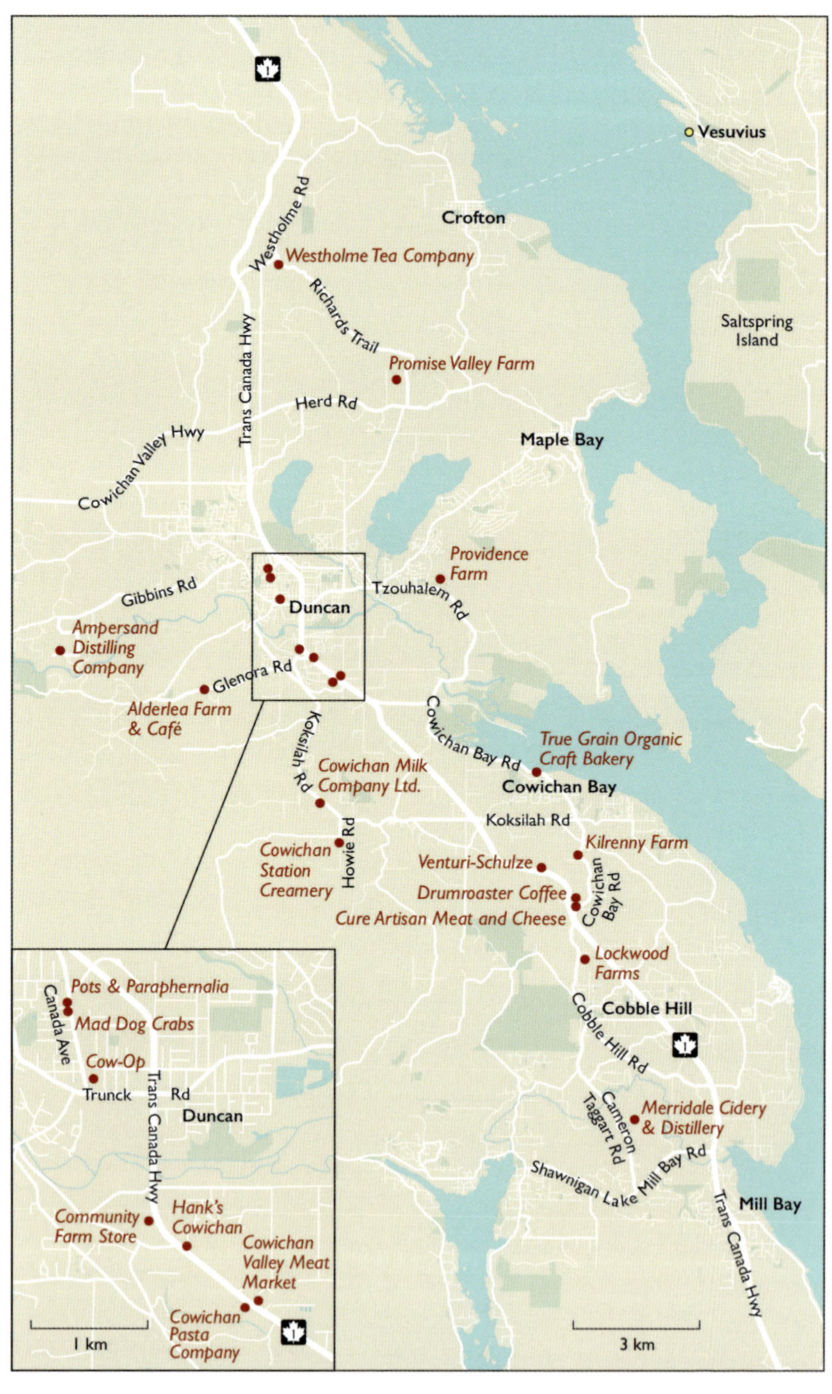
Vesuvius
Crofton
Westholme Rd
Westholme Tea Company
Richards Trail
Saltspring Island
Trans Canada Hwy
Promise Valley Farm
Herd Rd
Cowichan Valley Hwy
Maple Bay
Providence Farm
Gibbins Rd
Tzouhalem Rd
Duncan
Ampersand Distilling Company
Glenora Rd
Alderlea Farm & Café
Koksilah Rd
Cowichan Bay Rd
True Grain Organic Craft Bakery
Cowichan Milk Company Ltd.
Cowichan Bay
Koksilah Rd
Howie Rd
Cowichan Station Creamery
Kilrenny Farm
Venturi-Schulze
Drumroaster Coffee
Cure Artisan Meat and Cheese
Cowichan Bay Rd
Lockwood Farms
Cobble Hill
Cobble Hill Rd
Cameron Taggart Rd
Merridale Cidery & Distillery
Shawnigan Lake Mill Bay Rd
Mill Bay
Trans Canada Hwy
3 km
Pots & Paraphernalia
Canada Ave
Mad Dog Crabs
Cow-Op
Trunck Rd
Trans Canada Hwy
Duncan
Community Farm Store
Hank's Cowichan
Cowichan Valley Meat Market
Cowichan Pasta Company
1 km

2

FOOD ARTISANS OF THE COWICHAN VALLEY

True Grain Organic Craft Bakery

1735 Cowichan Bay Road, Cowichan Bay | 250-746-7664
truegrain.ca | FB: True Grain Cowichan Bay

Bruce Stewart.

About a year after I moved to Cobble Hill, this bakery opened in Cowichan Bay and captured the palate of all nearby bread connoisseurs. Jonathan Knight was the young baker who moved there to pursue his dream of producing artisan and organic breads made the old-fashioned way: no preservatives, dough conditioners, or anything artificial, long fermentations and risings, and texture and flavour to die for. True Grain quickly built a loyal following that included me; I used to stop there every Saturday for a French or sourdough baguette and a loaf of multigrain or perhaps raisin bread. There are seasonal treats, and Christmas time is remarkable for the shortbreads, stollen, and special European-style cookies and pastries that are regular features on many holiday tables. Bruce and Leslie Stewart took over in 2007 and, along with co-owner Todd Laidlaw, have stayed true to Jonathan's philosophy of artisanal bread with some modern sustainability improvements. There are no plastic bags at the bakery, all takeout packaging is compostable, even the lighting in the bakery has been changed to LEDs. The Stewarts purchase as many local and organic ingredients as possible. Many of the different grains used are stone-milled on-site (you can watch the big German mill grinding away through a large window). All the flours used in the bakery are grown in and milled in BC. They made this possible by building relationships with BC farmers, convincing them to grow the specific grains they wanted to use in their operation that weren't really being produced in BC anymore, like spelt, emmer, Khorasan and rye. Bruce is quite proud of sometimes being able to sell a "5-mile loaf" when the Red Fife wheat, a heritage variety, is grown at a local farm, or the "35-mile loaf" when it is grown on a farm in Metchosin.

Well Bred

Chemainus | 250-246-2411 | wellbred.ca | IG: wellbredbakery

Mark Primmer's business card reads *well-bred. well-read. well-fed.* I can't argue with any of that. As long as you accept the pun in bred for bread, you'll be okay. You see, while Mark does make good bread, he is also well-read, having graduated from the University of Alberta with a major in English. You will find Mark most Saturday mornings at the Duncan Farmer's Market as he and his wife, Shannon Peck, deal with the usual line-up of customers willing and waiting to buy his breads and pastries. These are produced in a tiny former art studio in Chemainus, equipped with a vintage 1952 Hobart mixer. Here's how he describes it on his website: "Well Bred was founded in the spring of 2011 and occupies a 300 square foot converted art studio on the owner's property cohabited by a PhD scholared cat named Hoban, a neighbouring farm rescue and an occasional rogue raccoon." They don't have a storefront. Mark bakes full-time to sell his products Saturday morning in Duncan, and if you call or email you might be able to arrange a pickup at their roadside self-serve stand. How Mark got into baking is a long story, but after a less-than-stellar career in other jobs and a somewhat successful stint at playing the stock market, he is now doing exactly what he wants to do—baking great-tasting breads and pastries and having fun with words and language. Examples from over the years: The Flaming Fig, Bacon Killer Brownies, Loosely Muesli, and Lemon Trollop instead of the more mundane Lemon Tart. Spend some time chatting at his stand or reading his social media posts if you need some laughs. But at the end of all the puns and witty repartee in person the important part for me is at the end of his motto—well-fed.

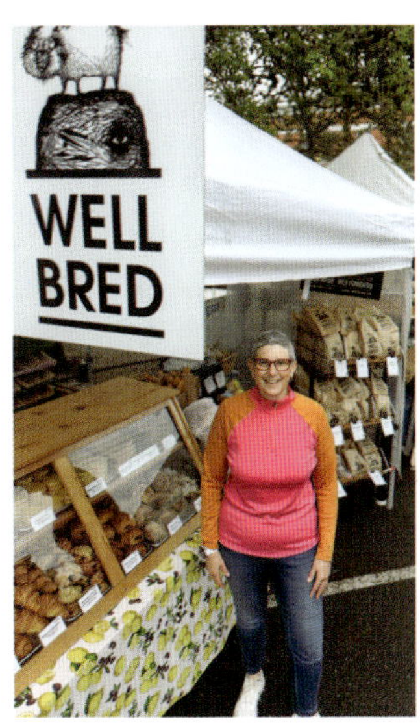

Shannon Peck.

Ampersand Distilling Company

4077 Lanchaster Road, Duncan | 250-999-1109
ampersanddistilling.com | IG: ampdistillingco

Ampersand Distilling Company got its start down behind the flower garden at Sol Farm just outside of Duncan in a small shed close to the raspberry bushes. From the start it's been a real family business driven with an intensity by late founder Stephen Schacht. Stephen and his son Jeremy started from scratch. They welded the stills together and built everything by hand. I saw the facility as it was coming together, and it had the whole air of "mad scientist" to it. But their unique approach has worked amazingly well. After the flagship product Ampersand Gin came Per Se Vodka, also a big hit with their loyal fans, not to mention a more unusual product called Nocino. It's made with green walnuts steeped in pure spirit, then spiced with lemon peel, cinnamon, and allspice to create a smooth Italian-style liqueur. These creations are made from 100 percent organic BC wheat and have garnered multiple awards over the years. Use of these products and others are inventively covered in Ampersand co-founder Jessica Schacht's cocktail book *The Five Bottle Bar.* The tasting room at the distillery is open by appointment only, but you can always find the "mobile" version of the tasting room on Saturdays at the Duncan Farmers Market.

Jeremy and Jessica Schact.

Merridale Cidery & Distillery

1230 Merridale Road, Cobble Hill | 250-743-4293 or 1-800-998-9908
info@merridale.ca | merridale.ca | FB: Merridale Cidery & Distillery

Janet Docherty.

When I first met Rick Pipes and Janet Docherty of Merridale Cidery, this husband-and-wife team was still experiencing the growing pains of purchasing an old cidery that, as the realtors probably put it, "had lots of potential." One day I arrived during a cider apple "crush" day, when Rick was practicing new-found electrical skills in repairing a finicky switch, then used an old hockey stick to stickhandle apples up a rickety conveyor belt to the press, where old sheets of canvas, valued for their natural stores of beneficial yeasts, could rip apart at any time as they filtered the juice from the pressed apples. Things have changed much since then, as the dynamic duo, along with their son Jason, have pushed ahead with project after project for the cidery, which is so popular it gets thousands of visitors each year. There's the bistro, the covered patio, the tasting room, and the gift shop featuring "Merridale Makes" products like jams, jellies, and chutneys. There are orchard and cidery/distillery tours, private parties, musical events, picnics in private areas of the orchard, and you can even book a stay in one of two yurts perched by a peaceful pond. And then there is the Brandy House. In June of 2013, Merridale obtained the first artisan distiller's license in the province, a breakthrough in provincial liquor legislation that makes it possible for smaller distilleries to actually make a profit on their products. Try the apple cider brandies.

Venturi-Schulze

4235 Vineyard Road, Cobble Hill | 250-743-5630
venturischulze.com | IG: vswine

Giordano and Marilyn Venturi moved to the Cowichan Valley in 1987, and since then, they and Marilyn's daughter, Michelle Schulze, have become well known for wines grown from grapes that are carefully selected for their unique microclimate and terroir. But you absolutely have to try their balsamic vinegar. It is made according to the tradition established hundreds of years ago in north-central Italy, in places like Modena and Reggio Emilia. True balsamic vinegar is made from grape juice which is reduced over an open fire, then aged for years and years in a series of special barrels made from different kinds of aromatic woods. A bottle of V-S balsamic vinegar is costly, no doubt about that, but I firmly believe it's worth it. The flavour is like nothing else you've tasted. A great deal of labour goes into growing the grapes; then there is the cost of the barrels, imported from Italy, and the time it takes before they have an authentic balsamic vinegar they can bottle—at least four to six years. Those "authentic" balsamic vinegars you can buy for five bucks a bottle at the supermarket these days are industrial products. They are made in Italy, according to standards, but the grapes are not organically grown; companies could make it overnight by quickly souring some alcohol and then adding colourings, sugars, and flavours. *Not* a traditional method. For special gifts, you can order the balsamic in a bottle hand-painted by a local artist, try the limited edition of maple balsamic, or the ultimate offering, balsamic vinegar that is over thirty years old.

Left to right: Marilyn and Giordano Venturi, Michelle Schulze.

Another Venturi-Schulze product that's not quite so expensive is verjus, which literally translates from the French as "green juice." Marilyn explains, "In our vineyard we thin out a lot of unripe grapes, and it seemed such a shame to just let them fall to the ground, so we started to collect them and crush them to make our own verjus, which we pasteurize and bottle." You can use verjus in your cooking to liven up a sauce or add it to cocktails or just to soda water for a nice little spritzer. It's tart, sweet, and refreshing all at the same time. Check their website for availability as it is often sold out. But you can also try their jams, many of which are made with balsamic vinegar and fruit that is either grown on their estate or picked locally.

Cowichan Valley Meat Market

5191 Koksilah Frontage Road, Duncan | 250-746-8732
cowichanvalleymeatmarket.com | FB: Cowichan Valley Meat Market

This butcher shop is the go-to place for quality and tradition for residents of the Cowichan Valley and also for many customers willing to make the drive over the Malahat. The shop is owned by the Quist family (in the valley since 1923), which supplies the shop from a large farm and abattoir it owns north of Duncan. This is where many of the animals that end up in the butcher shop are raised, on farm-grown forage with no hormones, so it's a great source of local meats, although the retail outlet has been so successful that the Quists source some of their animals from the British Columbia Interior, raised to their exact specifications. They are always happy to cut a steak or roast just the way you want it and have been working on a growing variety of in-house-cured meats. Even if you're just passing through from up- or down-island, don't miss picking up a package of their double-smoked bacon. Over the past few years, the shop has expanded its line of house-made deli meats and carries a number of other locally made products such as sea salt from the Vancouver Island Salt Company.

Island Farmhouse Poultry

Cowichan Bay | 250-746-6163 | farmhousepoultry.ca

Day Shift Workers at Island Farmhouse Poultry.

You will find Island Farmhouse Poultry products in Country Grocer, Quality Foods, Root Cellar, Red Barn, and independent grocers across Vancouver Island and the Gulf Islands. While the distinctive logo on the compostable package immediately tells you the chicken inside was raised and processed on the island, it doesn't give you the story about how the company came to be and why you should be backing a local hero. When the provincial government announced its intention to update meat inspection regulations, the almost immediate result was that a number of companies announced they would be shutting down. They either had no desire or not enough money to make the mandated changes to their operations. For Lyle Young of Cowichan Bay Farm, that meant he would have to ship his pastured chickens and ducks to the Lower Mainland for slaughtering and have them shipped back again for sale. Instead, he decided to build his own

» Island Farmhouse Poultry

processing plant to do his poultry and that of other area farmers. Island Farmhouse Poultry was the guinea pig for the interpretation of the new rules. Now owned by Rossdown Farms, Island Farmhouse Poultry still provides a valuable service to all sizes of poultry farms in the area, employing seventy local workers and supplying a high-quality air-chilled product to customers who want to know that the chicken they're cooking and eating was raised on Vancouver Island.

Cure Artisan Meat and Cheese

5–1400 Cowichan Bay Road, Cowichan Bay | 250-929-2873
curemeatandcheese@gmail.com | FB: Cure Artisan Meat and Cheese

Brad Boisvert.

Sometimes I think I could almost live exclusively on cured meats, cheeses, sausages, and all the condiments that go with them. Imagine my delight when Chef Brad Boisvert and his wife Leah opened a deli a five-minute drive from where I used to live in the Cowichan Valley. Most of what you can buy there has been made by Brad, including the fantastic cured meats—made from locally sourced animals whenever possible. Brad got hooked on the craft when he was in training at the Culinary Institute of America. Brad is always looking for balance, nicely provided through the textures of his chicken or duck liver pâté, terrines, a nice sausage, or smoked duck breast. And you can't forget the cheese. You'll find locally produced cheeses, and he imports some real rarities. Brad makes several of his own condiments, including three different types of mustard, a spicy ketchup, red onion jam, and beautiful little pickled quail's eggs. My secret fantasy? Accidentally being locked up inside Cure with no hope of rescue for a few hours.

Drumroaster Coffee

24–1400 Cowichan Bay Road, Cobble Hill | 250-743-5200
drumroaster.com | IG: drumroaster

Courtney Larkin and Carsen Oglend with dad Geir Oglend at the rear.

For most of the time I lived in Cobble Hill, the Drumroaster was my local. It was just a five-minute drive from my house, but I know many people who drive much, much farther to head to this café and roasting facility, and for good reason. First, the coffee. I love the taste of their espresso blend of beans. All the coffees at Drumroaster are ethically sourced. The second reason to go to the Drumroaster is for the service and baked goods. This all comes from the Oglend family. Geir Oglend founded Drumroaster after spending more than thirty years in the coffee business. His wife, Patricia, oversees all the baked goods. Carsen Oglend heads the roastery and training centre next door. Daughter Courtney Larkin is a barista extraordinaire who also educates new staff. This may be at the Drumroaster or somewhere else on the island, as the Oglends also roast coffee beans to order for many cafés and restaurants as well as supply and repair their espresso machines. The Oglends have also greatly expanded the selection of all the equipment and accessories you need to make your own best coffee at home. Years after moving to Victoria, I almost always bump into someone I know at the Drumroaster when I visit, which speaks to the dedicated following the Oglends have built and the quality of their products and service.

Westholme Tea Company

8350 Richards Trail, Duncan | 250-748-3811 or 1-855-748-3811
westholmetea.com | IG: westholme_tea

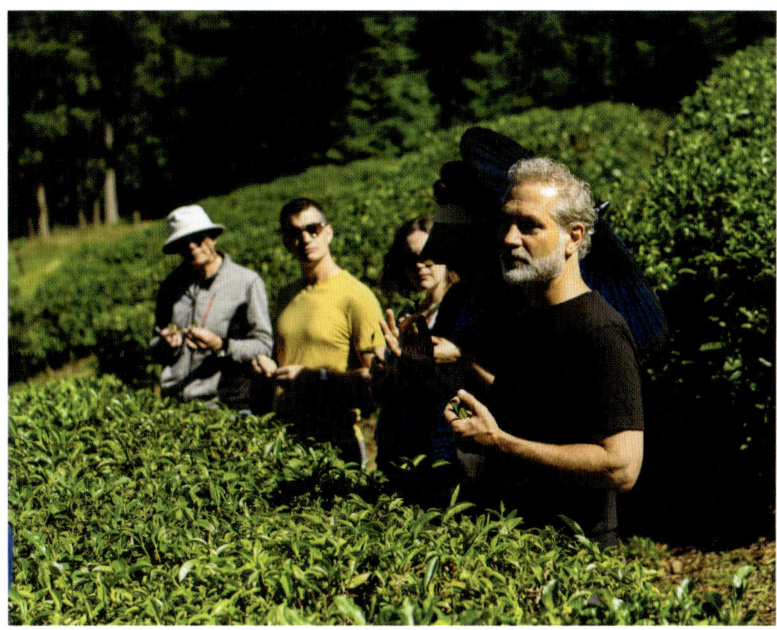

Victor Vesely (right) giving a tour of the Westholme Tea plantation.

This is the home of one of the only farms in Canada growing tea plants and actually harvesting tea. More about that later. When I first visited the Westholme Tea Company in North Duncan it was called Artfarm, since many of the original products being sold there were Margit Nelleman's works of pottery. Margit Nellemann and Victor Vesely moved to Vancouver Island to live their dream of combining a farm with a gallery and tea shop. I was drawn there by Margit's teapots. They reminded me of the artistic style in the animated Beatles movie Yellow Submarine: elongated pour spouts, bulbous belly-like pots, whimsical tops, elaborate

» Westholme Tea Company

designs painstakingly etched by hand. As Artfarm evolved into Teafarm, Margit and Victor decided to import fair-trade teas from around the world in an effort to keep artisan tea growers in business. Then, Victor started the painstaking task of creating a tea plantation. Most of the time, the climate in the Westholme Valley is favourable to the *Camellia sinensis* tea plant. But heavy snow and freezing temperatures can easily set back or even kill the plants. Those planted in 2010 survived their first deep freeze, and now the plantation is up to about eight hundred plants. It took years before there were enough leaves to harvest, since you only harvest the new, top leaves of the plant each year. Finally, each year Westholme releases a small quantity of their Westholme Terroir Teas. Don't worry if you visit and they're out of stock. There are many other teas to try at the farm shop. And I often meet Victor at the Duncan Farmers' Market to see what he has brewed up for market-goers to sample. One favourite of mine is Westholme's traditional Earl Grey tea made with a base of Assam tea before a true Italian cold-pressed, organic oil of Bergamot from Calabria is added. They make other blends with locally sourced or organic mint, chamomile, stevia, stinging nettle, and calendula. They have also developed blends of teas to reflect the character of people born under Chinese zodiac signs. I'm a Dog, and I love my signature blend. Tours of the tea plantation are available but must be booked in advance.

Pots & Paraphernalia

863 Canada Avenue, Duncan | 250-748-4614
potsandparaphernalia.ca | IG: potsandpara

One of the larger kitchen and bath shops north of Victoria, this two-storey collection in a beautiful brick heritage building has been in business for over forty years and is strong on all the popular kitchen cookware, bakeware, and dinnerware brands as well as kitchen appliance lines including Breville and Dualit toasters. You'll also find some intriguing edibles, like flavoured oils, sauces, spice rubs, olives, bitters, and soda syrups. Sometimes walking into a shop like this can be intimidating because of all the different selections, but whenever I've been there, the staff has always been both friendly and knowledgeable, and that goes a long way these days!

Pots and Paraphernalia owner Terry Raven.

Cowichan Milk Company Ltd.

4590 Koksilah Road, Duncan | cowichanmilk.ca | IG: cowichanmilk

Left to right: Matthew, Darbi, Margie, and Ben vanBoven.

The land that the Cowichan Milk Company sits on today has been in use as a dairy farm since the late 1940s when William Inglebright developed the land. Lumber from the property was used to build a big barn, which still stands today, albeit with a steel-sided covering. The great-great-granddaughter of William Inglebright is a veterinarian in the Cowichan Valley who helps care for the cows at today's dairy operation, which has been owned by the vanBoven family since 1960. Herman and Ida vanBoven had seven children, and their son Ben now owns the farm, and he and his wife, Margie, and their son, Matt, run the farm with occasional help from Matt's wife, Darbi. The vanBovens are among a growing number of BC dairy farms who are using robotic machines to milk the cows, which allows the cows to be milked any time they feel like getting milked and spares the farmers from getting up very early each morning for scheduled milkings. You can buy milk, chocolate milk, and coffee cream in reusable bottles directly at the farm, but the vanBovens launched a home delivery program just before the Covid-19 pandemic and haven't looked back. They had started out with the idea of just delivering milk, eggs, and bread. But when the pandemic hit, all the farmers' markets and many shops had to close their doors. Many of them came to the Cowichan Milk Company to see if they could help deliver their products to their customers. Now, via their website, you can choose from over seven hundred Vancouver Island products to have delivered to your door, anywhere from Ladysmith to Mill Bay. It's like having an old-fashioned milkman, but today's version can deliver a lot more than your weekly supply of milk.

Cowichan Station Creamery

4354 Howie Road, Duncan | 250-710-3007
cowichancream.ca | FB: Cowichan Station Creamery

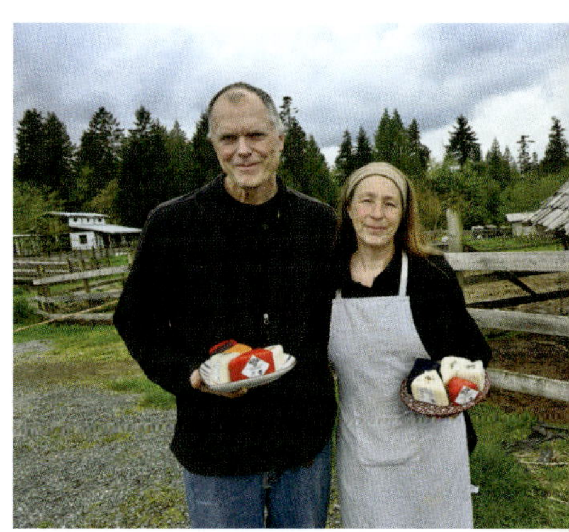

Henry Rekers and Renee Davy.

In a first for Vancouver Island, you can put your money into a vending machine, make a selection, and out will pop a fist-sized hunk of locally made cheese that has been carefully dipped in wax to preserve all of its goodness. At Cowichan Station Creamery, Henry Rekers and his wife, Renee Davy, run a small herd of dairy cows and specialize in making cheeses (except for their fresh curds) from unpasteurized milk that are aged a minimum of sixty days. Many of the cheeses are alpine in nature, with Gruyere, Emmental, Gouda, cheddar, and jack styles being made, but with whimsical names and nods to local place names like Koksilah, Tzouhalem, and Prevost. Henry told me they prefer to dip their cheeses in non-toxic food safe paraffin wax because it is a better preservative, keeping out air which could spoil the cheese. They add some dried petals or seeds as decoration on the top of each block. They have a variety of cows that they milk on the farm but are slowly leaning toward increasing the number of Gyr cows in the herd. The Gyr is an Indian breed originating in the state of Gujarat, but there are Gyrs available for breeding and dairy purposes in North America. Henry says their volume of production is lower, but they are very heat tolerant, and their milk is high in fat which makes for very good cheese. You can watch the cows via their website live cams that overlook the barns, milking parlour, and the front pasture where they get some sun and exercise. And the vending machine? Henry says you'd be surprised at how many people will knock on your door at all hours demanding cheese. This way they can just pop their cash or cards into the machine 24/7 to get their fix.

Promise Valley Farm

7088 Richard's Trail, Duncan | 250-746-7579
promisevalleyfarm.ca | IG: promisevalleyfarm

For Mark and Caroline Nagtegaal, Promise Valley Farm isn't their first go-round at dairy farming, but it is the first one where they feel that they have total control over the products they produce. They have chosen to run a herd of exclusively Guernsey cows as they are a breed easy to work with and give milk of superior quality with high butterfat and protein content. These cows produce something called A2A2 milk that, for some people, is easier to digest. Promise Valley is certified organic and the Nagtegaals practise regenerative agriculture, which means they keep adding nutrients back into the soil. Mark says building quality soil is where it all starts, producing the grasses the cows thrive on. The cows are on the pasture from spring through fall and silage from the grasses the farm stores for use over the winter. The milk is processed right there on the farm, and you can buy it at the farm store from a milk dispenser using your own container or their signature glass bottle. The milk is non-homogenized, so when it settles it has some wonderful cream on top, the same cream top you get on their yogurt, which is available more widely at retail shops in plant-based packaging you can compost. The yogurt is rich and smooth and comes in Vanilla Bean, Lemon, Honey, and Balkan style.

Mark and Caroline Negtegaal and (right) Caroline with a friendly member of the herd.

Alderlea Farm & Café

3390 Glenora Road, Duncan | 250-597-3438
alderleafarm.com | FB: Alderlea Farm & Cafe

This is a British Columbia-certified biodynamic farm not far from Duncan in the Cowichan Valley. John and Katy Ehrlich own the farm, and it certainly fits the description of bucolic. The front yard is home to gnarly, decades-old heritage apple and plum trees that still groan with loads of fruit. Spend a few minutes walking around to the back of the farm, and you'll soon discover a wonderful view, down a steep hill into a green-swathed pasture with grazing animals and extra plantings of veggies. John feels strongly about having people come to the farm, especially with their children, to see how things work and is more than happy to explain the concept of biodynamic farming. In addition to the actual growing of vegetables, the Ehrlichs now supply over two hundred families with vegetables through their community-supported agriculture program, which runs from May through December. People come once a week to pick up the share of that week's harvest paid for at the beginning of the season; this helps John with the upfront costs of each year's plantings. Then there is the café at the farm, open seasonally, where people can have a coffee and lunches or early dinners made from farm-fresh produce. The café is now run by Marley and Ruby, John and Katy's son and his wife. They've expanded the outdoor seating area, which is one of the nicest places in the Cowichan Valley to enjoy a farm-to-table dining experience.

Katy and John Ehrlich.

Lockwood Farms

3805 Cobble Hill Road, Cobble Hill | 250-252-3447
lockwoodfarms.ca | IG: lockwoodfarms

When I lived in Cobble Hill, I used to see James and Cammy Lockwood at their stall at the Duncan Farmers' Market every Saturday, and I would load up on their fresh veggies and their eggs . . . if they had any left. The eggs are still one on their most popular products as you can find them in many small retailers in Victoria and beyond. Their farm, with a lot of very hard work, has expanded over the years to become what used to be a standard model of Canadian agriculture, the mixed-use farm. There are chickens and pigs and a wide variety of vegetables and fruits all being grown together, instead of the monoculture model many larger farms have subscribed to. You can't call it "old-style," though, as some very modern methods are used to create a much more sustainable and ethical product. Smaller machinery is used, like wheelhoes and seeders (my dad used to use those in our garden) and landscape fabric that can be reused for years, cutting down on weeds and the labour it takes to control them. When it comes to Lockwood Farm "Eco Eggs," a company called Enterra takes waste from produce (fruits and vegetables) that is created even before it reaches the consumer and feeds it to black soldier flies who create tonnes of larvae. Those larvae are then dried and added to the feed the Lockwoods give to their chicken, not to mention the other benefits the chicken get from being pastured rather than caged, and so on. In spite of their busy lives with farm chores and family, you're still likely to see one of the Lockwoods at the Duncan Farmers' Market once their first vegetables of the season arrive in the spring and right through to the fall harvest.

Cammy and James Lockwood.

Providence Farm

1843 Tzouhalem Road, Duncan | 250-746-4204
providence.bc.ca | FB: Providence Farm

Some of the participants in Providence Farm programs.

The history of Providence Farm goes back to 1864, when the Sisters of St. Ann purchased 160 hectares of land near Duncan, building first a home for young First Nations girls, then one for orphaned girls from St. Ann's Academy in Victoria. Over the years the property has served as a school for both boys and girls, but since 1979, the farm and its spectacular, metal-roofed main building have housed a great number of community services under the auspices of the Vancouver Island Providence Community Association. While therapeutic programs for those facing challenges are at the heart of Providence Farm, the production of food plays a major role. The market garden provides many kinds of produce and bedding plants that are sold at the farm store as well as at various farmers' markets in the Cowichan Valley. Providence Farm is herbicide, pesticide, and antibiotic free. Heritage breeds of chickens are free range and double as Animal Assisted Therapy pets! Vancouver Island University offers agricultural workshops at the farm including classes on backyard bee and chicken keeping. The late James Barber, also known as the Urban Peasant, was a big fan of the farm, and the wood-burning oven behind the main building turns out excellent pizzas and is dedicated to his memory.

Cowichan Pasta Company

H1–4970 Polkey Road, Duncan | 250-732-2457 | cowichanpasta.com

The Cowichan Pasta Company is the brainchild of Chef Matt Horn. Travelling through Italy and seeing so many shops selling fresh pasta convinced him that we needed that kind of choice on Vancouver Island. Matt makes both extruded pastas and stuffed ravioli, which he used to make painstakingly by hand until he managed to afford a machine. He uses only Vancouver Island ingredients, including salt from Vancouver Island Salt Company, Cowichan Valley beef, British Columbia spot prawns, and vegetables and foraged items like seaweed and chanterelle mushrooms with the seasons. Even the flour comes from Vancouver Island-grown hard wheat that is milled at True Grain Organic Craft Bakery's mill. Matt stresses that you don't need fancy sauces to complete the experience when you're eating his pastas; you don't want to overwhelm their delicate flavour. You can order from Matt online or find a growing list of shops that carry his products on his website.

Chef Matt Horn.

Kilrenny Farm

1470 Cowichan Bay Road, Cowichan Bay | 250-743-9019
kilrennyfarm.com | FB: Kilrenny Farm

When I moved to Cobble Hill from Vancouver, it wasn't long before I met Deborah and Russ Fahlman, buying fruits and vegetables from the Fahlmans' organic farm and booth at the farmers' market. Then they fulfilled a decades-long dream of making pasta for sale when they finally took the plunge to renovate their farm-gate shop into a commercial kitchen, bought an Italian extruder pasta machine, visited Italy once again to learn more about making pasta, and started cranking it out. I love their malfadine, a ribbon of pasta that is ruffled along the edges and really holds the sauce, such as Deborah's marinara made from tomatoes grown on their property. Along with egg-based pastas, Deborah also makes spelt and kamut pastas, which are lighter on the gluten factor.

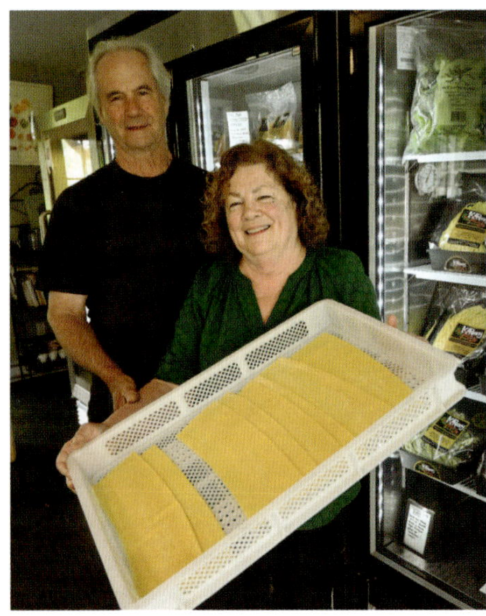

Russ and Deborah Fahlman.

Triple Smoke Foods

Shawnigan Lake | 672-202-3338 | triplesmokefoods.com
FB: Triple Smoke Foods

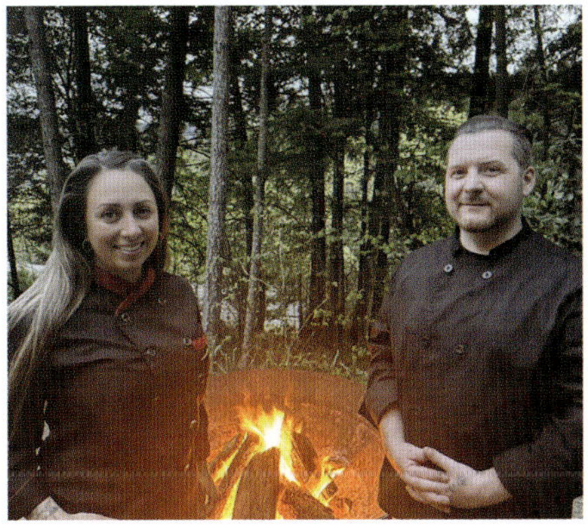

Natasha and Jake Townsend.

Learning about how people got into artisan food businesses is always fascinating. And I love a story that starts, "It all began when . . ." For Jake Townsend of Triple Smoke Foods, it all began when his wife Natasha gave him a smoker for his birthday. So, couple a new smoker with an already-ingrained love of campfire cooking, and the experiments with smoking spices began. They wanted to be able to bring that smoky flavour indoors, and putting the smoke into spices people already use seemed like a good way of doing it. Triple Smoke Foods debuted in 2014, and they've increased the number of products they offer from six to fifteen. You may see other smoked spice products with "smoke flavour" on their list of ingredients, but Triple Smoke uses real woods like applewood, hickory, and mesquite to smoke the spices before grinding and blending, with no artificial additives. There are lots of recipes on the Triple Smoke website to give you ideas of how to use the products. The pouches and jars let you keep them fresh, but the recipes should mean you use them more often! What I really like are two relatively new products that Jake and Natasha have developed that seize upon the chili crunch foodie craze, a smoked chili garlic onion finishing oil, and their smoked ginger garlic chive finishing oil. Use their spices or rubs to cook your food, then give them a splash of this stuff and you'll be in *sitting 'round the campfire* heaven!

Mad Dog Crabs

775 Canada Avenue, Duncan | 250-715-0206
maddogcrabs.ca | FB: Mad Dog Crabs Fresh Seafood

Scott Mahon.

I first met Scott and Katie Mahon at the Downtown Duncan Farmers' Market when it used to be in the old train station parking lot every Saturday morning. Scott was a commercial fisherman who would bring a big cooler full of crabs to their Mad Dog Crabs stall with one or two lonely crabs burbling away in an aquarium for show. Every now and then, along with my crab, he would try to sell me a big chunk of octopus arm from the octopuses he would sometimes have to wrestle off one of his crab traps. I always said no, but that was before I grew a little more adventurous in my cooking. The "crab shack" became so popular that Scott stopped fishing, and he and Katie opened a stand-alone seafood shop not far from downtown Duncan and now sell fish and crabs caught by his fisher colleagues. You'll also find a selection of smoked fish products and ready-made foods you can take home to eat like tuna pot pies, smoked salmon quiche, crab cakes, and chowder from a secret family recipe.

Hank's Cowichan

Unit 3–5311 Trans-Canada Highway, Duncan | 250-597-7727
hankscowichan.com | IG: hankscowichan

It's getting harder and harder for me to drive up-island from Victoria these days. I'm not talking about the traffic, although that often can be a pain, it's just the number of great places there are to stop and shop and snack on the way. Take Hank's Cowichan, conveniently just off the Trans-Canada Highway on the way into Duncan. Formerly an empty industrial office space, the trio of partners in Hank's carved a commercial kitchen and cozy café into existence that offers coffee roasted by co-owner Dana Meiner of Peaks Coffee, high-quality baked goods and breads from chef-owner Aaron Walsh, and amazing "provisions" from Aaron's wife and chef-owner Louise Pickles of Pickles' Pantry. Her duck confit, chicken liver parfait, and pork terrine quickly found a way past my palate and into my heart. The co-owners met at their respective stalls at the Duncan Farmers' Market and decided to join forces in a brick-and-mortar location. And the Hank of Hank's Cowichan? Louise told me he was an elderly loyal customer at the market who passed away just before Hank's opened. Now his name lives on in the business but also in Louise and Aaron's dog named Hank.

Dana Meiner, Louise Pickles, and Aaron Walsh.

Community Farm Store

2–5380 Trans-Canada Highway, Duncan | 250-748-6227
communityfarmstore.ca | IG: communityfarmstore

Left to right: Nicolette Genier, Anisophia Genier, Julian Bjornson, Cara Bjornson, Cyrus Genier.

The Community Farm Store (CFS) began life in 1993 as an organic farm market and bakery in rural Duncan. When I moved to the Cowichan Valley, it had relocated to a somewhat cramped warren of aisles and floor to ceiling shelves in the Duncan Garage building. It became my go-to place for all the good things I couldn't find anywhere else. I'm talking a wide range of certified organic products, from emmer (an ancient grain) to products like hazelnut oil, with a bonus of fresh, local organic produce in season. The dried-foods section had no rival in the area, and still doesn't. In fact, it's even larger since the store relocated to a building just south of Duncan with ten thousand square feet of space. While it looks much more like a traditional grocery store now, owner and president Nicolette Genier says the CFS mandate remains the same: provide food and other products that are both good for the community and good for the planet. That means all products are organic and as local, ethical, and fairtrade as possible. The CFS also offers a membership plan that gets you discounts on bulk purchases and other benefits to help ease your grocery bill in exchange for your loyalty, but you don't have to be a member to shop there.

ONLINE FARMERS MARKET
COW-OP

Cow-Op

360 Duncan Street, Duncan | 250-999-3134 | cow-op.ca | FB: Cow-Op

Even though I live in Victoria, I can still shop nearly one hundred different farms and food vendors in the Cowichan Valley from my desk, then take a short drive downtown to pick it all up. The Cow-Op is a non-profit farmer and food processor co-operative that started operation in 2015 and has been growing ever since. The concept is simple. Go online, choose what you want to order from the weekly offerings of various vendors, and enter your credit card. If you live in the Cowichan Valley there are a number of depots where you can pick up your orders. Here in Victoria, for a small delivery fee, I take my own boxes or shopping bags to my designated pick-up depot and transfer the goodies waiting for me there to my boxes or bags, and I'm off. If I've ordered something that needed to be refrigerated or frozen, the staff at the depot retrieve it for me, and off I go. In the past, I've ordered fresh baking from True Grain Organic Craft Bakery, Mexican spice blends from Duncan-based Ixim Foods, even bedding plants for my vegetable garden. It's a perfect solution: farmers and food producers save time by delivering to just one location while serving multiple customers, and buyers can shop a large number of products from the convenience of their computers, year-round.

Cow-Op employees Tamra Nash and Laura Boyd-Clowes.

SATURDAY SOJOURN

My day in the Cowichan Valley always starts with cappuccino and a baked treat at **Drumroaster Coffee** in Cobble Hill. It's just off the Trans-Canada Highway at Cowichan Bay Road, leaving you with a conundrum: carry on to Duncan, or amble down the hill to Cowichan Bay? Because it's market day, head straight to Duncan and the farmers' market centred on City Square. It's open year-round, and even in the winter you'll find fresh baking, artisan food products, and plenty of conversation with the vendors. If you've frittered away your time and feel peckish, you want to stop just south of Duncan at **Hank's Provisions**. The freshly made sandwiches there, along with your second coffee of the day will keep you going. From Hank's dart back into Duncan but turn right on Trunk Road, which turns into Tzouhalem Road, and before you know it, you're at **Providence Farm**. As you turn into the long driveway, you'll see the main building with its gleaming metal roof. Park there and make your way into the back area, where you can see fruit trees, the community gardens tended by seniors, the plant nursery with anything you need for your garden, and the farm shop featuring foods produced on the farm.

Follow the curves to Cowichan Bay, pick up a baguette or other baked goods at **True Grain Organic Craft Bakery**, and you're probably well into mid-afternoon. If you need to chill out, head to **Merridale Cidery & Distillery** on the other side of the highway for a casual cider tasting or even stay for dinner at the bistro.

Mid-Island

- Bowser
- Buckley Bay
- Coombs
- Errington
- Fanny Bay
- Ladysmith
- Nanaimo
- Nanoose Bay
- Parksville
- Port Alberni
- Qualicum Beach
- Tofino

3

1704

MID-ISLAND

When you look at it from tip to tail, Vancouver Island is pretty long. And it's not exactly narrow, either. Our mid-Island region in this book is more like the middle of the south part of the island. This chunk of the island takes in the eastern region from Buckley Bay near Denman Island and south to around Ladysmith. Then head west to places like Coombs and Port Alberni all the way out to the west coast with Tofino and Ucluelet perched on the edge of the Pacific Ocean. I know the stretch of the Trans-Canada between Cobble Hill and Nanaimo quite well, for in the early years of my move to Cobble Hill, I was still going back and forth a lot to Vancouver via the Departure Bay–Horseshoe Bay ferry. The best advice I have to give about that region is to get off of the highway as much as you can when you're not in a hurry (actually sometimes getting off of the highway is the best way to avoid traffic jams slowing you down). There are always the beautiful murals in Chemainus to distract you, and you really must get onto 1st Avenue in Ladysmith for a whole string of wonderful food places, bookshops, and antique markets. If you like sci-fi on TV like I do, you will recognize some of the streets in downtown Ladysmith as backdrops for the *Resident Alien* series. There are some great farms in the Cedar/Yellow Point area, and I never miss the Cedar Farmers' Market if I am passing through area on a Sunday. Many of the vendors you find at Saturday markets both north and south of Cedar make a point of attending the Cedar market on Sundays, and the famous Crow and Gate pub is in that area. If you want to make believe you are in an old English country pub complete with that kind of menu, this is the place to do it. It's been there since 1972, and was the first officially designated "Neighhourhood Pub" under BC Liquor Law Legislation.

Getting out to Vancouver Island's west coast is a must for everyone who comes to this province. The drive through the Alberni

Valley to get to Tofino and Ucluelet is right up there with my top ten drives in BC . . . yes, it is twisty and curvy and up and down, but think about what it was like up until the early 1970s when it was just an unpaved logging road. While Tofino and Ucluelet still offer up a bit of laid-back hippie vibe, the food and drink scene is becoming more and more sophisticated with some very good chefs willing to spend at least a few years putting down roots and encouraging other chefs to work there as well. I do recall, though, that the very first chef at the "new" Wickaninnish Inn was not fond of the foghorn that often blew through the night off Chesterman Beach when he was trying to get some sleep. Well, one person's annoyance is another person's romance, I'd say.

Catie's Hot Dilled Beans
Dorman Rd
Corcan Rd
19A
Qualicum Beach
Island Hwy
Lowry's Rd
19
Memorial Rd
Inland Island Hwy
Little Qualicum Cheeseworks
Parksville
Eat Fresh Urban Market
4
Alberni Hwy
Coombs
Old Country Market - Goats on the Roof
BoMé Cheese
4 km
Natural Gift Seafoods
NW Bay Rd
Stewart Rd
Island Hwy
Qualicum Beach
Weinberg's Good Food
2nd Ave
Beach St
Memorial Rd
Berwick Rd
Meat Craft Island Butchery
Wild Culture Bakery
500 m
Weinberg's Good Food
Buckley Bay
Deep Bay
Stellar Bay Shellfish
Island Hwy
Inland Island Hwy
10 km
Qualicum Beach
Coombs
To Tofino
Port Alberni
Nanoose Bay
Ladysmith
Island Hwy
The Worldly Gourmet Kitchen Store
Gateacre St
Old Town Bakery
1st Ave
100 m
Nanaimo
Yellow Point Rd
Yellow Point Cranberries
Ladysmith
1
Wild Culture Bakery, Meat Craft Island Butchery
Hammond Bay Rd
Metal Rd
Rutherford Rd
Bodhi's Artisan Bakery
Island Hwy
Nesvog Meats
Bowen Rd
Estevan Rd
Nesvog Meats
Jingle
Pot Rd
Esquimalt Vermouth Company
Nanaimo Pkwy
Nanaimo
St. Jean's Cannery
10th St
3 km
McLean's Specialty Foods
Fitzwilliam St
Terminal Ave
Front St
Bastion St
Commercial St
Flying Fish
Cold Front Gelato
150 m
River Rd
Johnston Rd
The Salty Woodsman
Stamp Ave
500 m
Port Alberni
Bedford St
Wild Flower Bakeshop & Café
3rd Ave
Argyle St
Tofino
Naas Foods
500 m
Campbell St
Industrial Way
Picnic Charcuterie, West Pacific Seafoods

FOOD ARTISANS OF THE MID-ISLAND

Bodhi's Artisan Bakery

5299 Rutherford Road, Nanaimo | 250-585-6015

Bodhi's Artisan Bakery is tucked into a small collection of buildings off a traffic circle in North Nanaimo called the Boardwalk on Rutherford. Bill Clay founded Bodhi's there in 2008. Before that he was a long-time pastry chef who fell into baking when he was asked to teach it to culinary students at Vancouver Island University. When you walk into Bodhi's (the name for a tree where Buddha attained enlightenment) you get a warm, rustic feeling from the wood floors and walls. You'll find loaves there like fig hazelnut, sourdough, garlic asiago, and multigrain. And because of Bill's pastry background, you can enjoy what he calls "World Class" cinnamon buns, chocolate croissants, and a savoury whole wheat croissant with pesto cream cheese, asiago, caramelized onions, roasted red pepper and basil. Bill's croissant dough recipe was given to him and the other members of Team Canada Baking Team from the 2008 French National Team when they travelled to Paris to put on a demonstration at a European bread exposition. If the French give you a recipe like that, you use it, and Bill has to good advantage at Bodhi's.

o **Bill Clay.**

Old Town Bakery

510 1st Avenue, Ladysmith | 250-245-2531
oldtownbakery.ca | IG: oldtownbakeryladysmith

Baker Chelsea Tunnell.

There has been a bakery in the same location on 1st Avenue in Ladysmith since the 1930s. City Bakery was the first name, then Alexander's Bakery, and from 2002 on, Old Town Bakery, the first venture into Ladysmith for founders Kate and Geoff Cram. When you're thinking of a stop in Ladysmith going up or down the Trans-Canada Highway, don't just pull over for gas, get off the highway and onto 1st Avenue. Then follow your nose to Old Town Bakery. The bakery has become known for its cinnamon buns, but you can't just call them cinnamon buns. There is usually a new style of bun featured every month and the hardest part of stepping into the shop is usually facing nine different trays of buns and trying to figure out which ones to order. Last time I was there I couldn't decide so tried four types. On Saturday mornings they may pump out up to 96 dozen buns. That's 1,152 happy people. Or if they were all like me and ordered four at a time, 288 happy people. The bakery is also a great stop for coffee and tea, and don't ignore the cakes, pastries, and breads, either! If you want to shop gluten-free baking, you head to the Crams' Wild Poppy Market just down the street at 541 First Avenue. Gluten free grab-and-go meals and baked goods are made in house daily. There's a small eating area with counter service, and you'll also find locally made food products from up and down the island and gluten free staples. What, no ice cream? No worries, go next door to Old Town Ice Cream at 539 First Avenue, open seasonally and featuring gelato from the Crams' Cold Front Gelato shop in Nanaimo.

YOU MIGHT ALSO WANT TO TRY:

- **Wild Culture Bakery**, 692 Bennett Road, Qualicum Beach (wildculturebakery.com). I spent a marvellous afternoon there a few summers ago. You drive up a long, gravel driveway and pick your way through carefully tended lawns and flowerbeds to get to the bakery. There's a covered patio where we sat with tea and pastries listening to local musicians playing gentle tunes just a few feet away from us.

- **Wildflower Bakeshop & Café**, 5047 Argyle Street, Port Alberni (cafewildflower.ca). Cozy with great pastries, coffee, and patio. It should be. It was created by two experienced hospitality workers with over thirty years of experience in top restaurants and hotels.

Esquimalt Vermouth Company

3091 Jingle Pot Road, Nanaimo | 778-835-8146
esquimaltvermouth.ca | IG: esquimaltvermouth

Quinn and Michela Palmer.

Michela and Quinn Palmer started their relationship with beverages back in 2015, when they made Rootside Provisions soda syrups from fresh and whole ingredients, not artificial "flavourings." They also love drinking vermouth and other aperitifs, but in BC there aren't a lot of options to be found on liquor store shelves. What they had learned making the syrups stood them in good stead when it came working with fortified wine, the base of vermouth and aperitifs, and they start by making their wine from fermented BC honey. Like many of the artisans in this book, they weren't born to their current careers. Michela was a sales rep for a fashion distributor, and Quinn was in polling and research. Working in the hospitality industry helped to support them while they developed Rootside Provisions. As time went on, they learned more and more from bartenders and seminars about flavours and ingredients they were excited about and focused on creating products that really stood out. I love how their labels echo the old-style European aperitif design but always with the addition of seagulls, since the business was founded in Esquimalt, home of many, many seagulls. In 2024, they uprooted Rootside and Esquimalt Vermouth and moved to Nanaimo where they built a new facility but have also started beekeeping so they can supply their own honey and grow some of the botanicals that go into making their variety of fortified wines.

Their bestselling Rosso and Dry Vermouths each won the designation of World's Best Vermouth at the World Vermouth Awards in the Semi-Sweet and Dry categories in 2023. Then there's a category of unique aperitifs called Cascadia, flavoured with 100 percent botanicals native to this region. They were the first producer of quinquina (tonic wine) in Canada since the Second World War!

Meat Craft Island Butchery

6461 Metral Drive, Nanaimo | 250-933-2257
690 Berwick Road South, Qualicum Beach | 250-594-0889
meatcraftbutchery.ca | IG: meatcraftvanisle | IG: meatcraftqualicum

Kerry Martini was running a successful Meat Craft butcher shop in Port Moody, but Vancouver Island was calling her home. So together with her business partner Sean Austin, they opened Meat Craft Island Butchery in Nanaimo, and not long after that, another outlet in Qualicum Beach. The first time I went by the shop in Nanaimo was just days after they opened, and Kerry told me they had sold three hundred pounds of sausages on opening day. It seems Nanaimo needed a shop like theirs! Meat Craft pays a lot of attention to where they source their beef, pork, chickens, and lamb, and they start as local as possible. When you run down the list of farms on their website, you'll see some familiar names like Tannadice Farm from Courtenay, Hertel's from Port Alberni, and Twin Rivers Farm from South Nanaimo. Kerry says they know most of the farmers and visited the farms to see their operations before taking them on as suppliers. Kerry is originally from Nanaimo. She was working in sales in the Lower Mainland but found herself driving two hours back and forth to get the kind of quality meat she wanted. That's how the Port Moody shop got started. Bringing local quality meat to folks back home in Nanaimo seemed like a natural progression. Today's modern butcher shops like Meat Craft know that today's consumers like convenience, so they always have ready-made burgers, kabobs, marinated meats, and even a

Kerry Martini.

» Meat Craft Island Butchery

base for Shepherd's Pie to get you started. The other thing a butcher shop gets known for is its sausages. Judging by the three hundred pounds sold on opening day, Meat Craft has it nailed. They commonly rotate around forty different sausage recipes for the shops. I talked with one of the sausage makers there who told me he had already been at his craft for over a decade and was proud that there are no fillers or preservatives in his sausages, but that he is a big fan of using beer from local brewers as a binder, which he says works far better than water. I'll drink to that!

Nesvog Meats

1533 Estevan Road, Nanaimo | 250-753-4248
2139 Bowen Road, Nanaimo | 250-758-3611
nesvogmeats.ca | FB: Nesvog Meats and Sausage Co.

In 2023, Nanaimo landed in the top five of the fastest growing cities in Canada. So maybe it's not surprising I'm telling you about another two butcher shops in the city. These two are owned by the same family and are just three kilometres apart. Arnold and Ingrid Nesvog met when they were both teenagers working at the Nanaimo Co-Op. He swept the floors, while she was at the deli counter. Eventually they married, had children, but then the Co-Op closed. Opening a meat shop was the first idea they had to solve the employment problem. In his years at the Co-Op, Arnold had become a top meat cutter, and Ingrid had the deli experience, so it was a natural solution. That was in 2005, and in 2014 they purchased another butcher shop and made it their second location. All three of the Nesvogs' sons work in the business, and their wives are active in it as well. The Bowen Road location is more of a grab-and-go kind of shop with pre-made vacuum packed meals, while the Terminal Park location on Estevan Road is more of a full-service store. Like most of today's independent butcher shops, Nesvog is a place to go to find locally raised meats and poultry, and they source produce used in their operations from local farmers as much as possible. And yes, they even make so-called *turduckens*—a roast consisting of a chicken, inside a duck, inside a turkey. I've heard about these for a while . . . time to try one?

Left to right: Connor, Arnold, Cameron, Josh, and Ingrid Nesvog.

Picnic Charcuterie

700 Industrial Way, Tofino | 250-889-5738
picniccharcuterie.com | IG: picnic_charcuterie

Dani Simons and Robyn Lord.

Picnic Charcuterie sprang into existence in 2014 with Tina Windsor at the helm. She learned the butchery and cured meat trade while working at the now-shuttered Choux Choux Charcuterie in Victoria. Current owners Robyn Lord and Dani Simons took over at the beginning of 2023, both having worked in restaurants and kitchens for over a decade. Picnic has become the place for take-out charcuterie boxes from their retail outlet. They've also taken on more large-scale event catering as well as partnerships and collaborations with other local restaurants and vendors. Even with the greater emphasis on catering services, they remain committed to producing their charcuterie by sourcing top quality meats from local farms that practise the highest animal welfare possible and traditional farming methods. But . . . their unique sea salami sources from the ocean, not the field, using locally harvested smoked bull kelp and chilli. Another tasty offering is grass-fed beef or bison bresaola seasoned with locally foraged herbs and dry aged for four to eight weeks. The charcuterie platters aren't just cured meats, however. They include BC and imported cheeses, house-made preserves and spiced nuts, pickles, olives, and fresh bread. These are a few of my favourite things . . .

Flying Fish

180 Commercial Street, Nanaimo | 250-754-2104
flyingfishnanaimo.ca | FB: Flying Fish Nanaimo

I first met Flying Fish owner Glen Saunders while I was working in Prince Rupert in the late 1980s. He was working in his family's trucking business and hosting fabulous dinner parties out of a little cabin he rented at Lakelse Lake. But I soon learned about his retail savvy when he bought an old house in Terrace and renovated it into a much-needed kitchen, bed, and bath shop. Then he did the same thing in Prince Rupert with his Cow Bay Gift Galley, and then again in Nanaimo with Flying Fish. Glen found Flying Fish a great home in the historic A.R. Johnston & Co. building in the heart of downtown. You can call the mix of goods in Flying Fish eclectic if you must, but I love Glen's large wall of kitchen gadgets and the corresponding shelves full of other much-needed kitchen accessories and decor items. And if you walk into the nearby furniture section, you can find unique dining room tables and chairs as well; it's where I found my sustainable mango-wood dining room table.

Left to right: Scott McLeod, Gina Moscrip, and Glen Saunders

The Worldly Gourmet Kitchen Store

522 1st Avenue, Ladysmith | 250-245-7307
worldlygourmet.ca | IG: zworldlygourmet

The first time . . . wait, check that, the *second* time—because they had expanded the size of the shop in between my visits—I walked into the Worldly Gourmet Kitchen Store in downtown Ladysmith, I was truly amazed. I couldn't figure out how they managed to fit such a vast collection of pretty much every facet of cookware possible into a relatively small space. And what was it doing in Ladysmith? Go back a few decades. Lebanese immigrants Kamal Saab and his wife, Therese, had been living in Toronto, with Kamal carving out a new career in office supplies since he couldn't find work in his first career in hospitality management. On a business trip to Vancouver Island, he fell in love with the mountains and beaches. He moved immediately there with his family. In 2014, they were ready to start their own business, and the original owner of the Worldly Gourmet was ready to sell. They both love cooking, and love exploring techniques and ingredients from around the world, so the name of the shop remained, but then they started restocking it, and restocking it . . . and to this day they are constantly on the lookout for new merchandise. But useful stuff, not gadgets that don't really work. "If it's not here you don't need it," is their motto on Instagram.

Kamal Saab.

If you simply walk the aisles of the store without stopping to look at anything, you'll spend eight minutes there, I measured it with my video camera. But if would defy anyone to spend so little time there, even if you're not a kitchen gear nerd like me. What I have been most impressed with is the breadth of their collection. There aren't just a few aprons to choose from, there are dozens. Gripstand bowls? Multiple sizes, multiple designs. Into breadmaking? They have several sizes of those banneton baskets to proof your dough. But how can they make this huge inventory work in a town of just around ten thousand people? Therese told me the customer base for their shop ranges all the way from Victoria to far up-island and people from the Lower Mainland even make a point of stopping there. It helps that they are both so helpful and knowledgeable about everything they sell.

BoMé Cheese

1876 Alberni Highway, Coombs | 250-586-2663
bomecheese.ca | FB: BoMé Cheese

Sure, the star of the show in Coombs is the Old Country Market with the goats on its roof, but if you drive a couple of kilometres past the market and hang a right onto the long driveway just past the U-Haul and Island Self-Storage lot, you'll find yourself at BoMé Cheese. The company was founded in 2016 by Horst Boehm and Bibi Menge (you can see where the name came from) who came to Canada from Germany complete with dairy equipment and restaurant furniture from a hotel Bibi had owned. From the café on the top floor of the building you can enjoy some traditional German cuisine like schnitzel, goulash, and spaetzle, and peer down through a huge window to the cheese making operation and see the cheese makers in action when milk from local farms is brought in to be processed. Many of the cheeses are mountain alpine style, and they have fun with the names, like Coombozola (instead of Cambozola), Brie Happy, Bomarti (instead of Havarti), and so on. They even make a mountain cheese with hemp called Up in Smoke. The cheese is made using only fresh milk from grass-fed local dairy cows. Horst is a civil engineer who specialized in building food processing plants in several countries and ran his own goat dairy farm and cheesery in Germany. Bibi was a chef and restaurant management in the Swiss Mövenpick Group and a long-time owner and manager of her own hotel complete with a café and restaurant. Bibi's son Jonas is the assistant cheese maker, and through his technical studies has modernized the cheese making process to cut down on water and energy consumption. It's a trio of experts who have put together a winning combination of food and hospitality.

Bibi Menge, Jonas Menge, and Horst Boehm.

Cold Front Gelato

306 Commercial Street, Nanaimo | 250-591-7719
coldfrontgelato.com | IG: coldfrontgelato

Cold Front Gelato began life in Nanaimo in 2018, but by 2022 the entrepreneurs behind Ladysmith businesses Old Town Bakery, Old Town Ice Cream, and Wild Poppy Market had bought in, a decision Kate and Geoff Cram say "just felt right, the stars seemed to align, we were in the right place at the right time. It complements the other businesses beautifully while maintaining its own individuality." That individuality means specializing in making innovative gelato flavours while respecting Italian tradition of using local, fresh ingredients. One thing they are trying to emphasize as the years go by is widening their range of local products and ingredients to incorporate some real BC traditions and tastes. That means a rhubarb-based gelato in the spring and something crazy like Leprechaun Tracks around St. Patrick's Day, created with a fresh mint gelato base layered with white chocolate almond bark, marshmallows, mint chocolate ganache, and chocolate *stracciatella*. Along with new monthly flavours, Cold Front offers vegan and gluten-free scoops and pints, and customers like me love the aroma of freshly made waffle cones when you walk in the door.

Geoff and Kate Cram.

Little Qualicum Cheeseworks

403 Lowry's Road, Parksville | 250-954-3931
cheeseworks.ca | FB: Little Qualicum Cheeseworks

Albert Gorter, Chelsea Enns, and family.

Little Qualicum Cheeseworks is another of my favourite family businesses that grew out of a small idea and kept growing and growing. Nancy and Clarke Gourlay began their cheese business in 2001, and in 2004, they moved it to Morningstar Farm, where they built their herd of Holstein, Ayrshire, Brown Swiss, and Canadienne dairy cows. Sadly, Clarke Gourlay passed away in 2019, and Nancy decided to retire in 2021. But the Gourlay family sold it into the good hands of another experienced dairy duo, Albert Gorter and Chelsea Enns. The farm and cheeseworks continue with over a dozen different cheeses, and the farm itself is a must-visit if you're in the area. There is a very well-stocked farm-gate store that is open six days a week. You can also do self-guided tours of the farm to watch cows being tended to by a robotic milking machine and observe the cheese making process. And don't miss the fresh milk dispenser. Bring your own container or buy the bottle there, insert coins or tokens, and fill! The milk is pasteurized but other than that it is pretty much the closest thing you can get other than straight from the cow.

Yellow Point Cranberries

4532 Yellow Point Road, Ladysmith | 250-245-5283
yellowpointcranberries.com | FB: Yellow Point Cranberries

Grant Keefer.

Most of our cranberries come from farms in BC's Lower Mainland or even the eastern United States, but there is a cranberry farm right here on Vancouver Island, busily pumping out fresh and processed cranberries. From a distance, Yellow Point Cranberries just looks like a flat, green field. But in the fall, you can walk right into the field and see all the beautiful red berries hidden in the little bushes. Owner Grant Keefer says he and his wife, Justine, started this farm because of his childhood. He grew up surrounded by cranberry farms in the Fraser River delta; when they moved to Vancouver Island, they found a piece of land that was perfect for cranberry farming, so they did what came naturally to him. The Keefers produce many different cranberry concoctions in a commercial kitchen on the farm and sell them in their cute little retail shop, the Cranberry Cottage. The cranberry salsa, cranberry horseradish jelly, and cranberry amaretto peach butter are all very tasty. There's even a cranberry mustard. The Keefers offer guided tours of the farm in September and October. If you can't get out to Yellow Point, the good news is that they do a few farmers' markets up- and down-island, selling fresh cranberries for Thanksgiving, and they are available in a number of grocery stores. Online shopping is available year-round. Grant notes that they want to be careful with expansion. "We don't want to get too big," he says. "We just want people to be able to come out and visit the farm, learn about cranberries, and of course try some of our fabulous cranberry products."

Barrelhouse Brine

Nanaimo | 604-354-5635 | barrelhousebrine.ca | IG: p1cklebaron

Joel Wilson.

Joel Wilson started playing around with fermenting pickles back in 2015 in East Vancouver. He does fresh pack pickles and kosher ferments, which is all about the salt and not using vinegar. Since moving to Nanaimo, he has been growing his business, for which he wants to use Vancouver Island cucumbers. However, the weather doesn't always co-operate with his farmers, and he can run short. When life hands you lemons, you make lemonade. For Joel, life handed him pineapples, available year-round. Some Jamaican friends told him about pickled pineapple salsa, and it has become a great standby for him, a sweet version and a sweet-and-*hot* version made with habanero peppers. Another product Joel has recently developed is his Barrelhouse Sourback Cocktail Brine. It's made from the juice left over from his kosher dills and is much in demand from bartenders and mixologists. When Joel told me his booth won best cocktail at Victoria's Art of the Cocktail event in 2023 with his Pickleback Shot, I had to admit I didn't know what that was. Simple: a shot of good whiskey followed by a shot of pickle juice. In this case, Joel's brine was made with a locally made Nanaimo beer, and his garnish was a fermented cucamelon, a tiny fruit that looks just like a miniature watermelon and had a watermelon/cucumber flavour. The theme of the Art of the Cocktail in 2023 was Las Vegas, which is why the photo of Joel you see here shows him going full Elvis with a giant pickle.

Catie's Hot Dilled Beans

2005 Dorman Road, Qualicum Beach | 250-927-5194
catieshotdilledbeans.com | IG: catieshotdilledbeans

There are certain food groups I can't do without. Chocolate. Cured meats. Pastries. Pickles (I know, they're not the real food groups but whatever). Pickles and preserves are what you get a lot of choice in when you deal with Catie's Hot Dilled Beans. The beans, of course, were her first product and what really launched her pickling career. Catie Grandmont was a piano teacher. She took the summers off teaching but had learned how to make pickled beans and other delights from her Hungarian mother back home in Argyle, Manitoba. Here on Vancouver Island, she made those beans to take to summer parties. They were so good people wanted more. Soon she was supplying four local bars and restaurants as her beans made a great upgrade from celery sticks in Caesars and Bloody Marys. The next step was getting her own commercial kitchen built on her property, and then Catie's husband, Michael Macdonald, stepped up and built her a wonderful little cottage that serves as her retail shop right beside the kitchen. When you visit on her Friday and Saturday openings, you can look through the window and see the pickling and preserving and jam-making by Catie's employees. Whether you find her at the shop or a market, Catie is happy to explain how all of it is done and how all the berries for her jams (except blackberries) come from the Qualicum area and how she supports local farmers as much as possible. Her husband didn't stop with the cottage. He built Catie's wheeled Pickle Shack that goes with her when she sets up at farmers' markets. I like how Catie has come up with a line of innovative pepper jellies that are based on her original jalapeno but then branch off into individual flavours featuring raspberry, blueberry, cranberry, and garlic too.

Catie Grandmont.

Islanders Fresh Authentic Mexican Sauce

Nanaimo | 778-269-2922
islandersfreshauthenticmexican.com | IG: islanders.mexican.salsas

What I like about the ever-widening Canadian cultural mosaic is when people come to settle in Canada from other countries, they invariably bring their food culture with them. Then they adapt their cooking to the ingredients they find here. Lily Rechon-Reguet grew up in Mexico City with a grandfather in her household who made all the salsas. As a child, she had no interest in observing the salsa making. Even as a teenager, she never helped make it. But when she first moved to Vancouver in her early twenties, she missed all those wonderful flavours. Luckily, she worked in the food service industry in Vancouver and also when she lived in France. When she came to Nanaimo, she was ready to start recreating those flavours. The first time I tasted her Sassy Tomato Fresh Salsa, I was blown away by how fresh and flavourful it was, and yet it came from a tall, elegant jar. You will only find her products at her retailers in refrigerated showcases. She wanted to make sure her customers could relive her experience growing up with these flavours. They contain no sugars, no preservatives, and are vegan and gluten free as well. Lily sources her jalapeño peppers from Vancouver Island when they are available, mostly later in the summer, but also relies on those grown in the Okanagan and Fraser Valley. She has three types, the aforementioned Sassy Tomato, the Savoury Jalapeño, and Spicy Lovers . . . which is really spicy but still packed with flavour. Her sauces have a refrigerated shelf life of four to six months, but don't worry, you definitely won't have it around that long. It could become a daily habit . . .

Lily Rechon-Reguet.

Louis Pasture Pork Crisps

Errington | primalsisters.com | IG: louispastureporkcrisps

It may sound like a cliché, but necessity really is the mother of invention. For Tamara Wensley, a trained nutritionist, health problems necessitated a change in her diet. Vegetarianism wasn't really working for her, so she decided to try paleo. But that meant giving up potato chips, and she loves potato chips. So Tamara and her sister Jennifer (who are known as "The Primal Sisters") started fooling around with a piece of pork skin and crisped it up. Their kids and the rest of their family loved the crisps, and they went into production by converting their father's old welding shop into a certified commercial kitchen. Like many other artisans, they started selling at farmers' markets and offering different flavours like you would find in potato chips—the original crisp with just salt, salt and vinegar, barbecue, and dill. Now bags of Louis Pasture (a great play on the famed Louis Pasteur) pork crisps are available in more than eighty stores around British Columbia. They have added new flavours and products like jalapeno cheddar, white cheddar, pork cracklings, beef chips, and Gingy—a pork crisp flavoured with ginger, orange peel, Himalayan pink salt, rosemary, black pepper, paprika, and honey powder, which makes for an amazing combination. The staff prepare everything by hand and fry the crisps in lard (pork fat). Skin and fat are two by-products of pork production that are often just thrown away so they're saving landfill space and adding value while creating a delicious, healthy product. The crisps are ketogenic, gluten free, preservative free, gelatine rich, and a bag provides eight grams of protein per serving. Why are they called The Primal Sisters? The story is told on their website: "Well 'paleo' is shorthand for 'paleolithic.' Primal is a nod to this 'caveman' lifestyle and way of eating. When we asked our parents' opinion on the name, Dad said: 'Primal Sisters makes me picture girls swinging in the trees.' We Love It!! Haha, thanks Dad."

Tamara Wensley.

Naas Foods

630a Campbell Street, Tofino | naasfoods.com | IG: naasfoods

Stevie Dennis is an Ahousaht member of the Keltsmaht First Nations and growing up in Tofino means he has spent his whole life on and around the ocean. While he is a commercial fisher, Steve also co-founded Naas Foods with the idea of sustainably harvesting kelp from the ocean and turning it into "flavour enhancers" you can use on a large variety of foods. The unadulterated Tofino Kelp Flakes have a natural saltiness from the ocean and provide a lot of umami, that mysterious fifth taste that goes beyond salty, sweet, sour, and hot to provide more flavour. The smoked kelp flakes are also made from dried bull kelp hand-harvested from the Clayoquot Sound but then smoked using salvaged wood chips from local sawmills. With more snack-style flavours, Naas also offers a Popcorn Seasoning and an Everything Seasoning. Along with the kelp products, Naas Foods runs a seafood shop seasonally in Tofino, where fresh fish and shellfish procured from local Indigenous fishers are offered for sale, and where sport fishers can take their catches to be processed and frozen for transport. If you're staying in the area, Naas has also put together ready-to-cook meals you can pick up featuring halibut, salmon, crab, prawns, and shellfish or a DIY oyster platter or tuna sashimi or "seacuterie," a mix of smoked and cured chinook salmon and specialty canned seafoods. It's one of the best ways to enjoy seafood caught locally by local fishers . . . and for Stevie it's a natural way to help make a community by striving to employ both members of his own nation and those of neighbouring nations.

Stevie Dennis out on the ocean.

Tofino Hot Sauce Co.

Tofino | 250-884-0654 | tofinohotsauce.ca | IG: tofinohotsauce

Lise Richard.

Lise Richard grew up in Nova Scotia . . . surfed the cold Atlantic waters there, and decided she wanted to try surfing the cold Pacific waters off Tofino. After some time spent working with her background in environmental science in Nanaimo, she went to Tofino one more time and stayed. She started working full-time in a restaurant. That was 2018, and in early 2020 the Covid-19 pandemic hit. While Tofino wasn't exactly a bad place to spend the shutdown, she started thinking about hot sauces—part of her job at the restaurant was making batch after batch of lime-cilantro sauce. So in the middle of the pandemic shutdown, she started the Tofino Hot Sauce Co. Lise was raised learning how to do canning and food processing, and she loved putting food in jars. When her mother learned about the company, she said Lise always thought she was "hot stuff" so her hot sauces should be called "Hot Tuff." I like the smooth consistency and textures that go along with her flavours. I also admire the labels devised for each sauce, which are a tribute to her Scottish grandmother, who used to tell her stories of sea sirens. Each mermaid on the label is different, with individual body shapes and hairstyles as well as personalities that match the heat of the sauce. The green mermaid is the "Hot Tuff" lime-cilantro stuff, her mildest sauce, the yellowy-orange mermaid represents the "Hotter Tuff" medium heat mango turmeric sauce, and the "Hottest Tuff" has a fiery red mermaid with the highest heat in a hibiscus tamarind sauce. Her latest product is a seasoning she makes by using the pulp leftover from the sauce-making process. Lise dehydrates the pulp, powders it, and mixes it with Vancouver Island Sea Salt. It makes a dynamite seasoning available in all three heat levels and an allspice-ginger flavour. I guarantee once you start using it you will start sprinkling it on everything.

Fanny Bay Oysters

Fanny Bay | 250-225-0125 | fannybayoysters.com | IG: fannybayoysters

The Taylor Family, owners of Fanny Bay Oysters.

One of the largest producers on Vancouver Island, this company exports its oysters and other shellfish products around the world. Fanny Bay Oysters was started back in the 1980s by three shellfish farmers and named after a bay in Baynes Sound, home to many BC shellfish farms. It's now owned and operated by Taylor Shellfish Farms, which started growing shellfish in Washington State's Puget Sound in 1890! Five generations later, Taylor family members are still intimately involved in all the businesses it owns. Fanny Bay Oyster products can be found in many retail outlets and restaurants, but the company also operates a small retail shop in Fanny Bay near the Buckley Bay ferry terminal at 1-6856 Island Highway South (250-335-1198). There is also a Fanny Bay Oysters seafood counter at the Old Farm Market in Courtenay at 660 England Avenue. And if you're visiting or from Vancouver, there's a Fanny Bay Oyster Bar and Shellfish market on Cambie Street in Yaletown, a casual yet upscale place to enjoy a fresh slurp.

Natural Gift Seafoods

1985 Stewart Road, Nanoose Bay | 250-954-7780
naturalgiftseafoods.com | IG: naturalgiftseafoods

Kingsley Bryce and Alistair Bryce.

Albacore tuna is one of my favourite West Coast fish. Ian Bryce of Natural Gift Seafoods has fished all kinds of species in a long career on the ocean, but albacore tuna is more lucrative these days. Ian was always getting requests from people he knew for tuna, so he would bring home some whole tuna. Then he decided to see how it would taste canned, so he had some done up, liked it, and started to sell that. Soon he had got into smoked loins, frozen whole loins, and smoked, canned tuna. I met Ian back in 2011 when he was still going out on his boat, but now he says he's boatless. "My sons Alistair and Kingsley are now each running their own boat. I guess that's okay after me being on the water for fifty years." Natural Gift Seafoods' albacore tuna is certified sustainable by both the Ocean Wise and Seafood Watch programs, and the entire albacore tuna fishery has certification from the Marine Stewardship Council. And albacore tuna is loaded with healthy omega-3 fatty acids. You can also get lingcod loins from Natural Gift, which make awesome fish and chips.

St. Jean's Cannery

242 Southside Drive, Nanaimo | 1-866-754-3191 | info@stjeans.com
stjeans.com | FB: St. Jean's Cannery & Smokehouse

Gerard St. Jean (third from left) helps celebrate the transfer of ownership of St. Jean's to the Nuu-Chah-Nulth Seafood Development Corporation.

St. Jean's has been serving commercial and sport fishers since 1961. The company started off very small, in the kitchen of Armand St. Jean, who practiced smoking oysters at home, ruining his wife's plants and smearing her typewriter ink on the homemade labels he stuck on plastic bags full of oysters he sold in local bars. Now they employ just over a hundred people in Nanaimo. Custom smoking of seafood is still a mainstay of the operation; many of the sport-fishing lodges up and down Vancouver Island send the catches of their clients to St. Jean's to be turned into lox,

» St. Jean's Cannery

hot-smoked salmon, or canned salmon. Eventually Armand's son Gerard took over as company president, and he told me he credits their small size and family roots as the reasons behind their longevity. They ship seafood all over the world and pack and smoke for large and small fishing companies alike. They offer dozens of products, including clam chowder, antipastos, pâtés, even canned wild chanterelle mushrooms. When St. Jean's celebrated its fiftieth anniversary, a new Nanaimo landmark was unveiled at the cannery: the world's largest salmon can, which doubles as a conference room and museum. Then, in 2016, ownership of St. Jean's was transferred to the Nuu-chah-nulth Seafood Development Corporation which represents five West Coast First Nations from the Nuu-Chah-Nulth Tribal Council. On the announcement of the deal, Larry Johnson, Nuu-chah-nulth Seafood Development Corporation president, said the deal re-establishes his peoples' connection with their traditional livelihoods. The cannery has a large gift shop, which you should visit, and don't forget to have your picture taken beside the big can when you visit the cannery—it makes for one of those iconic Vancouver Island photos.

Stellar Bay Shellfish

7400 West Island Highway, Bowser | 250.757.9304
stellarbay.ca | FB: Stellar Bay Shellfish

I spent a few hours with Stellar Bay oyster farmer Keith Reid one day and learned more than a few things about growing oysters, while witnessing the ingenuity required to make a living as a shellfish producer. Keith isn't just a farmer—he's an inventor, a marketer, and a jack-of-all-trades who realized you can't sit still in the shellfish industry. Much of the equipment necessary to raise oysters successfully is custom-designed by Keith, and he also realized that having a well-branded type of oyster was important to his sales. That oyster is the Kusshi, a small oyster with a deep cup and strong shell. Its small size and sweet flavour makes it the ideal entry-level oyster for people nervous about swallowing raw shellfish. Stellar Bay shellfish are only available at restaurants and from wholesale distributors and some seafood shops like the Fanny Bay Oysters retail shop at Buckley Bay.

Keith Reid.

YOU MIGHT ALSO WANT TO TRY:

West Pacific Seafoods, 700 Industrial Way, Tofino (250-725-2244). This is the original location of West Pacific Seafoods. See full description of business under the shop's listing in the Saanich Peninsula section.

Eat Fresh Urban Market

164 Bagshaw Street, Parksville | 250-248-3007
eatfreshurbanmarket.com | FB: Eat Fresh Urban Market

Eat Fresh Urban Market Store Manager Brydon Short.

Clayton Baker had what he thought was a long enough career in the grocery business when he sold his Thrifty Foods franchise in Parksville, having worked in a grocery store since he was fifteen years old. But a few years after he retired, he found that neither the Thrifty Foods nor any of the other grocery stores carried the type of groceries he wanted to buy nor had the same level of service he remembered providing for so many years. So he bought a building pretty much right across from the Thrifty Foods and started Eat Fresh Urban Market from scratch in 2014. Today he says the business is still growing like crazy and one of the reasons is that he likes his store to feel like your pantry at home. Just go through and pick what you have and start cooking. To help you out he has a real butcher shop in the store and chefs to give you help with your cooking, or you can pick up something they've already made for you. There's a bakery and fish department too. He says he tries to keep the prices competitive while at the same time featuring not only local foods and products but imported cheeses from France and exotic meats as well. All of this in a 7,500-square-foot store. It's kind of an old reference now, but he thinks back to what Robson Street in Vancouver used to be in its heyday, a group of independent businesses catering to their particular audience. Except Clayton has put all those separate entities under one roof. The butcher, the baker, the fishmonger, and the greengrocer too.

McLean's Specialty Foods

426 Fitzwilliam Street, Nanaimo | 250-754-0100
mcleansfoods.com | IG: mcleans.specialty.foods

Eric and Sandy McLean have been presiding over the counter at McLean's for over thirty years now, but they still bring a youthful enthusiasm to their business and the products they sell. They are known primarily for their cheese counter, stocking over a hundred different types of cheese from all over the world. You'll also find an impressive selection of gourmet oils, vinegars, olives, truffles, pâtés, and much more. On one visit, Eric offered me a taste of an American-made prosciutto that had been getting raves in culinary circles. Who knew that you would be able to find something like that in a shop in Nanaimo, British Columbia? Due to Eric's Scottish heritage, you will also find a long list of goods from the British Isles and from elsewhere in the Commonwealth, like South Africa.

Eric McLean.

Old Country Market – Goats on the Roof

2326 Alberni Highway, Coombs | 250-248-6272
oldcountrymarket.com | FB: Old Country Market - Goats on Roof

I hadn't been to the Old Country Market (better known as Goats on the Roof) in Coombs for years. It used to be a favourite stop on my way to Port Alberni and on to the wonderful beaches at Tofino. In recent years, however, I found myself driving by as the surrounding area became more of a draw for tourists. But when my wife asked, "Goats, on the roof?", during a drive down-island, we made the quick detour off the highway. Goats still gambol on the roof, the kitschy shops are still there, but when we walked into the actual Old Country Market, I was blown away. The market had been expanded, with a separate kiosk up the lane for fresh, local produce, in case lots if you want. There are huge departments crammed with local and imported food ingredients, glassware, tableware, and wrought iron. There are long counters stocked with dozens of different kinds of cheeses, meats, pastries, and breads. You may think of grabbing a little plastic shopping basket to carry around, but save yourself some time, and start with a full-sized shopping cart. There's also a double-length ice cream counter to cut down on line ups in the busy summer hours, an eat-in café that also features an outdoor patio, which in good weather gives you an excellent view of what the goats are up to. Why are there goats on the roof? Back in the seventies when the original market building was constructed by Old Country Market founder Kristian Graaten, the Norwegian immigrant decided to put a sod roof into the design, a common feature of some of the structures in his hometown of Lillehammer. The grass grew long on the sod roof and the legend goes that, after a few glasses of wine, Kristian's son-in-law suggested they borrow some goats to mow it. The rest is history. Every year from spring to fall two or three goats live on the roof complete with a shelter for them, and they amuse the tourists just by being there, but also when they choose to peer down on you from their lofty perch. There is even a live YouTube feed of the roof on the Old Country Market's website.

○ **A goat . . . on a roof.**

The Salty Woodsman

5161 River Road, Port Alberni | 250-735-9666
thesaltywoodsman.ca | IG: saltywoodsman

I always admire people who can turn a bad situation into something good. During the Covid-19 pandemic, Nile Verbrugge and his wife, Nadine, needed a way of making some extra money. Nile has friends and family working in the seafood industry, so in May of 2020, they started selling their catch out of a freezer in their garage. Push ahead to December 2022, and they moved to a storefront and started to fulfill requests from their customers to bring in spices and sauces, and soon their shelves were also stocked with coffee, tea, honey, and more—with most of it sourced from local and other BC artisans. With the seafood as their first offerings, Nile reports customers seem to like the crab cakes and bacon-wrapped scallops on offer along with their focus on local first, then BC, then Canadian products for sale.

Nadine and Nile Verbrugge.

Weinberg's Good Food

6856 Island Highway South, Buckley Bay | 250-335-1534
3–221 W. 2nd Avenue, Qualicum Beach | 250-594-4100
weinbergsgoodfood.com | IG: weinbergsfood

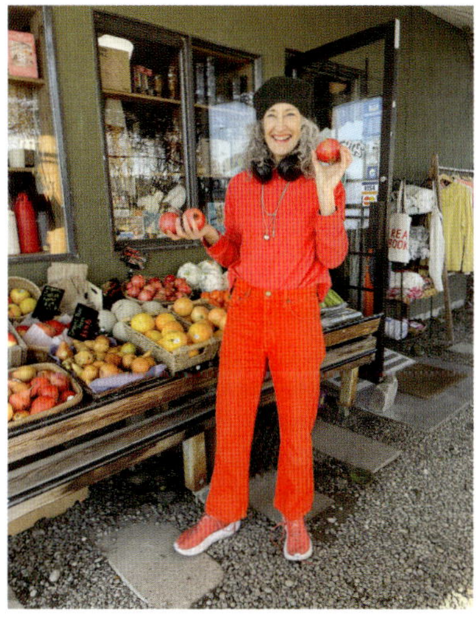

Leah Weinberg.

The first location of Weinberg's Good Food is a shop you barely expect to exist, tucked away under the back end of the gas station and sandwich shop at the Buckley Bay ferry terminal and next to the Fanny Bay seafood shop. But from the moment you go inside, you realize that it's not a typical convenience store for ferry passengers waiting for the next trip to Denman and Hornby Islands; it's a real grocery store that carries artisan products and baked goods from the immediate area as well as frozen meats like beef and lamb from local ranchers. As the salutation on its website used to say, "Sometimes missing the boat ain't so bad." Leah Weinberg created the store back in 2011 after she and her family had moved from Vancouver onto some family property in Fanny Bay. Suddenly she found herself miles away from easily buying simple staples like onions or apples. So she decided to restart a buying club she had been running in Vancouver. Club members put in orders, and then everything was delivered to one central location for pickup. The space at Buckley Bay just happened to come open at that time. That's when she realized she could serve a lot more people with a retail shop instead of a pick-up depot. At first there were tight restrictions on what she could sell as the convenience store upstairs didn't want to give up a share of the market for junk food and soft drinks. No problem. Leah brought in organic fruits and vegetables,

» Weinberg's Good Food

gourmet food items and BC-made charcuterie, along with a carefully curated selection of gift items for visitors headed to Denman and Hornby Islands for vacations. In 2019, the ownership of the building was about to change, and Leah and her husband, Gerald, decided to hedge their bets to find another location in case the new landlord wanted them gone. They found that second location at Qualicum Beach in a quaint collection of Tudor-style shops called Chilham Village. When they found out they could stay at Buckley Bay, they decided to open the other shop anyway. Leah says it took a while to figure out a different audience in Qualicum, but the charcuterie and deli items have proved to be very popular.

SATURDAY SOJOURN

Let's see . . . if I had a float plane or helicopter at my disposal, I could really come up with a fantastic Saturday Sojourn for Mid-Island. But let's assume I'm starting out in Qualicum Beach on a Saturday morning. Get an early start with a walk on the beach to greet the morning sun and work up an appetite, then off to the Farmers' Market, pick up a breakfast crepe or a pastry, coffee, and stroll around to visit the other vendors—shopping bags in hand, with a cooler in the car just in case. From the market, out to Coombs. Stop in at BoMé Cheese to pick up whatever cheese selection strikes my fancy then off to the Old Country Market nearby. Commune for a few minutes with the goats on the roof, then likely come out with a shopping cart full of vinegars, mustards, and perhaps some new tableware or bowls. Then it's a quick stop in Port Alberni for coffee and yes, another pastry, at the Wildflower Bakeshop and Café followed by a nice browse just down the street at Möbius Books. Did I mention there is also a bakery called Nook tucked inside the bookstore? Pick something up for the drive, or maybe to save for the next morning. Next stop is Tofino. You'll be hungry again because driving is hard work. Head to Picnic Charcuterie for say a mid-afternoon lunch? You can pick up a Picnic Platter for two to three people loaded with house-cured meats, gourmet cheeses, dried and fresh fruit, spiced nuts, pickles, olives, preserves, and a fresh baguette. Head to Chesterman Beach and indulge. Then go for another long walk on the beach because you'll need to work off all the pastries and picnic stuff. Check into your preferred accommodation and take a late afternoon nap. Dinner to follow at somewhere like Shelter, Wolf in the Fog, or a big splurge at the Pointe Restaurant at the Wickaninnish Inn. Return to your accommodation and sleep the sleep of the well-satiated. You can always diet tomorrow.

Greater Victoria

- Langford
- Oak Bay
- Metchosin
- Saanich
- Sooke
- Victoria

4

House-made
Cookies

GREATER VICTORIA

What can I say about this region? I've lived here for nearly ten years now, and I still feel like I've barely scratched the surface of all the places I want to visit and experience. According to census data from a few years ago, Victoria has the highest number of restaurants per capita in all of Canada: 4.6 restaurants for every thousand residents. That's a lot of places to eat. Restaurants come and go, however; and we lost some because of the Covid-19 pandemic, and still others are struggling with inflation and a difficulty in hiring staff. That being said, you'll probably never run out of new restaurants to try here, and the number of specialty shops has been steadily increasing as well. Everyone still wants to live here, and that puts a strain on housing, but there is no easy answer to that. I feel lucky to live here with the idea I am minutes away from being at the ocean and the mountains on the skyline. I love driving out to the farms in the Sooke-Metchosin area and picking up eggs likely laid that morning and am relieved that Sooke Harbour House has been reopened with a new crew dedicated to returning it to its former glory as a "local first" restaurant. Riding my bike down to Cadboro Bay has become a healthy habit although I do like stopping at Pepper's for some deli treats after I've been to the Moka House for a latte and baked good. That's okay, there's a big hill to climb on the way back. We have that mix of what travel writers call that "perfect blend of the old and new" with our parliament buildings and heritage buildings on Government Street and then the shiny new condos . . . but we've got some urban sprawl and traffic jams, too. Nobody's perfect.

3 km
The Market Stores
Parachute Ice Cream
Glenwood Meats
Langford
Sheringham Distillery
Galloping Goose Sausage Company
Metchosin
Nootka Rose Milling
Trans-Canada Hwy
Millstream Rd
Goldstream Ave
Sooke Rd
Veterans Memorial Parkway
Happy Valley Rd
Metchosin Rd
Lindholm Rd
500 m
Burnside Rd
Douglas St
Gorge Rd
Bridge St
Jenny Marie's Cracker Company
Damascus Food Market
Hillside Ave
Quadra St
Parachute Ice Cream
Rock Bay Ave
Working Culture Bread
The Wooden Shoe
Mile Zero Coffee Company
Bay St
Government St
Blanchard St
Phillips Soda Works
Maiiz Nixtamal Eatery
Silk Road
Deer and Dough Bakery Café
Wild Fire Organic Bakery
La Roux Patisserie
Fisgard St
Mexican House of Spice
Pandora St
Johnson St
Wharf St
The Tuscan Kitchen
Yates St
The Chocolate Project
Murchies
View St
The Market Stores
Broughton St
Fort St
Rogers' Chocolates
Farm + Field
Victoria Olive Oil Company
Crust Bakery
Dutch Bakery & Diner
Russell Books
Royal Oak Dr
Penna & Co. Kitchen & Giftwares
Macaloney's Island Distillery
Patricia Bay Hwy
Blenkinsop Rd
Root Cellar
Mckenzie Ave
Cedar Hill Cross Rd
To Langford (see inset above)
17
Fig Mediterranean Deli
Cedar Hill Rd
Sinclair Rd
For Good Measure
Pepper's Foods
Shelbourne St
Cadboro Bay Rd
Burnside Rd
Haus Sausage Co.
Dupplin Rd
Richmond Rd
Gorge Rd
Hillside Ave
Charelli's Cheese Shop
Craigflower Rd
The Local General Store
Foul Bay Rd
Fry's Bakery
Cook St
Bay St
The Market Garden
Catherine St
Fol Epi
GoodSide Pastry House
Spinnakers Gastro Brewpub
Cold Comfort Ice Cream Company
Fort St
Oak Bay Ave
Ottavio Italian Bakery & Delicatessen
The Whole Beast & The Village Butcher
Erie St
Finest at Sea Seafood Market and Food Truck
McLennan's Island Meat and Seafood
Niagara St
Dallas Rd
Root Cellar
For Good Measure
Beach Rd
1 km

4

FOOD ARTISANS OF GREATER VICTORIA

Crust Bakery

730 Fort Street, Victoria | 250-978-2253
crustbakery.ca | IG: crustbakeryonfort

Sherin Fernandes and Crystal Harris.

Crust Bakery was opened in 2013 by Crystal Harris and Tom Moore and quickly became well-known, named as Victoria's Best Bakery in at least one city publication. When I moved to Victoria in 2015 and my wife started working at Russell Books just up the street, it quickly became my go-to place for coffee and a pastry when I dropped her off for work. You know where Crust is as you approach because there are always people gathered in front of the shop window which is always full of their many and varied offerings. I'd say every tourist who has ever walked down Fort Street since 2013 probably has a photo of that window. And since 2020, Crust goodies can also be found at an outdoor kiosk at Uptown Mall in Saanich. There are certain things you can always count on, like the croissants and pain au chocolat, but the offerings also vary by the season and the bakers love to use fresh fruits in the pastries. Sherin Fernandes now co-owns the business with Crystal, and has been there almost since the beginning, taking on a baker role not long after she graduated from Le Cordon Bleu Pastry Program in Bangkok. Sherin is now quite happily making sure the kitchen behind the scenes at Crust runs smoothly, and she's always coming up with new items for the bakery and adjusting the regular stalwarts. She's very proud that everything in the bakery is made from scratch and that she buys local fruit in season to add authentic flavour to those limited time special treats. The individual tarts you can get at Crust are an easy way of taking care of dessert for a dinner party. Usually there are four to six different tarts, so I just buy a variety, with one for each person. It's then up to my guests as to whether they want to share! Don't shy away from trying the loaves of bread, either. We often get the multigrain to make sandwiches and if you're there on a Friday, check to see if they are still making the savoury croissant dough loaf which features bacon; you really can't stop eating it.

Deer & Dough Bakery Café

770 Fisgard Street, Victoria | deeranddough.ca
IG: deeranddoughbakery

Melinda Friedman always wanted to be a baker. Her first job in high school was at a bakery and ice cream shop, and she even spent her last year of high school at that shop on a Small Business Management internship. Then there was the other road taken. The Brooklyn, New York native decided to take a one-year course in filmmaking in Vancouver. She never left the BC coast, working in the film industry for thirty years in post-production, producing and directing. Then a project ended, pandemic hit, and she decided to move to Victoria ... and bake. First it was at her home in James Bay. She watched deer frolic in the neighbourhood from her kitchen window while she obsessed over pie dough and the company name was born: Deer & Dough. Melinda sold her baked goods to her neighbours. They liked it so much she opened a very small shop in Fairfield. We're talking 250 square feet—low overhead, but a big success. After eighteen months the lease was up, and she wanted to stretch her wings a little bit wider. Her new location on the Fisgard Street side of the Victoria Public Market building is proving a big hit with residents of neighbouring condos as well as nearby office workers. There's an outdoor patio and indoor seating at a bar wrapping around the tall windows with a cozy collection of tables and chairs under an airy ceiling. Melinda's most popular bakery items are coconut cake slices and a big cookie stuffed with dark chocolate chunks, pecans, and toffee. The café part of the operation features sandwiches, bagels, soups, savoury rice bowls, and comforting early morning porridge. The film producer turned baker has a big hit on her hands!

Melinda Friedman.

Dutch Bakery & Diner

718 Fort Street, Victoria | 250-385-1012
thedutchbakery.com | IG: dutchbakeryvictoria

It's a pretty unassuming storefront, but the number of people coming and going every day from it is impressive. These daily visits have been going on since 1956, when Kees Schaddelee arrived from the Netherlands with his whole family and rented a coffee shop on Fort Street. This turned into the Dutch Bakery & Diner and has remained family owned and operated ever since. The current owners, Jack and Brook Schaddelee and Michele Byrne are all cousins and grandchildren of Kees. Most of the children and grandchildren worked there at some point over the years. Since I moved to Victoria, it is one of my favourite places to buy two birthday cakes at a time since my wife and I share the same birthday and can't agree on which cake to buy. We often visit the diner with friends for a "coffee klatch" around 11:00 AM which usually includes a breakfast sandwich on a croissant or a very good Reuben. On one of my visits, Michele coaxed Jack out of the kitchen where he had been busy baking just some of the many pastries available from the refrigerated counter at the front of the shop. When I asked about the secret of their continued success, they said they owed it to their parents, who kept building a following over the years, and count families into their third and fourth generations becoming loyal customers. They like to keep the feel of the place familiar, and in the diner the walls are lined with photos of customers, workers, and the Schaddelee family from years gone by.

Jack Schaddelee.

Fol Epi Bakery and Café

101–398 Harbour Road, Victoria | 250-477-8882 | folepi.ca | IG: fol.epi

My first encounter with Cliff Leir of Fol Epi dates to 2004. I met him while he was toiling away at Wild Fire Bakery, getting ready to install an on-site mill that would help him grind forthcoming shipments of Red Fife wheat from one particular farmer in Saskatchewan. Those were heady days for Leir, who had gone from selling loaves baked in a self-built wood-fired oven in his driveway to being the main baker champion of Red Fife; he was trying to make sure this heritage variety of wheat, the granddaddy of many modern strains of wheat in Canada, wasn't going to fade into extinction. He told me how it was the best tasting wheat he'd found so far, with a subtle but much deeper, fuller wheat flavour. He was on to something. Red Fife made a comeback, and Cliff is still using it to bake some of his loaves at Fol Epi.

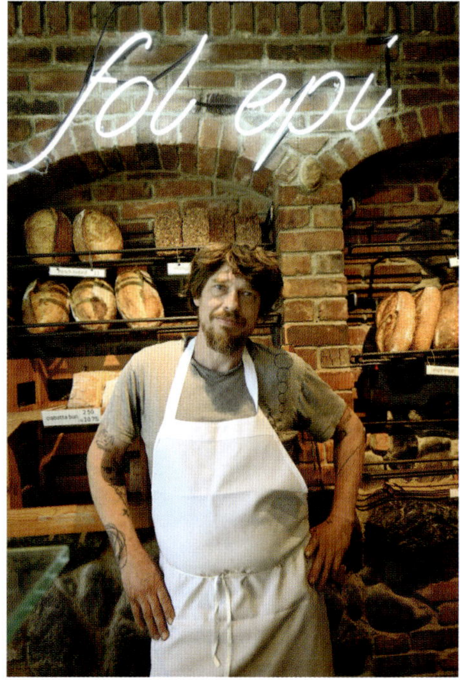

Cliff Leir.

Fry's Bakery

416 Craigflower Road, Victoria | 250-590-5727
frysbakery.com | IG: frysbakery

Byron Fry shaping loaves for the wood-burning oven.

Byron Fry was meant to bake bread. It's in his blood. His great-great-grandfather baked bread in Victoria at the turn of the twentieth century, and when Byron decided to bake bread in Victoria, the space on Craigflower Road that matched his needs was right across the street from the bakery operated by his ancestor all those years ago. Byron's present-day bakery probably doesn't look that different from the previous incarnation, from the chipped-paint and old-style chairs outside on the sidewalk to the wooden shelves holding the day's baking to the wood-fired brick oven. It was built in 2012, and it didn't take long for the bricks above the oven door to show a soot-stained patina from the thousands of loaves and pastries. Byron's breads are rustic and hearty, but his croissants and pain au chocolat pass my flakiness test, and people line up on Sundays for Pizza Day, featuring lots of great toppings.

GOODS

GoodSide Pastry House

1805 Fort Street, Victoria | 250-880-1540
goodsidepastryhouse.ca | IG: goodsidepastryhouse

I first met Haley Landa, co-creator of GoodSide, on the radio. She was turning up every few weeks on CBC's *North by Northwest* weekend morning show, enthusiastically sharing a recipe for some delicious, sweet creation listeners could recreate at home. I loved the smile in her voice and how she explained the recipes in a way that just made you want to make them. I was more than pleased when I heard Haley and her partner Curtis Helm, both experienced pastry chefs, had jumped the pond from Vancouver to Victoria and had secured a spot for the GoodSide Pastry House. It was even better when I learned it was going to be just a few blocks away from my house. I wasn't the only one who welcomed the idea of being able to buy Haley and Curtis's delights on a regular basis. When GoodSide opens for business, there are line-ups—those good kind of line-ups where people chat and discuss what they are going to buy once they get inside. While you can always count on excellent croissants and pain au chocolat, the other items at the counter change on a regular basis according to the seasons and what strikes their fancy. Always inventive and always scrumptious. If you are having a dinner party, a sure way to please your guests is to offer them individual GoodSide dessert creations, which are stunning in both presentation and flavour.

o **Curtis Helm and Haley Landa.**

La Roux Patisserie

519 Fisgard Street, Victoria | 778-265-7689
laroux.ca | IG: larouxlarouxlaroux

Chef Joanne Rodgers.

How does that old saying go? *Be careful what you ask for.* After twenty-five years working as a legal assistant, Rebecca Godin decided she wanted a change. So she retired and got a job as a barista, just to see how she liked the hospitality industry. That led to her moving to Victoria and starting La Roux Patisserie as a retirement project. "Now that I'm retired, I only work eighty hours a week," she says with a laugh. Rebecca didn't want to spend a lot of time in the kitchen at La Roux, but staffing difficulties during start-up meant she ended up there, which turned out to be invaluable experience in learning all facets of the operation. Now, she relies on Chef Joanne Rodgers to lead the creations . . . and they *are* creations. Every pastry and dessert is made in house, and when you combine the food with the décor, you might as well be in Paris. Customer favourites include the elegant Paris-Brest, a carefully layered combination of flaky pastry and praline cream.

Wild Fire Organic Bakery

1517 Quadra Street, Victoria | 250-381-3473
wildfirebakery.ca | IG: wildfirebakery

Wild Fire Organic Bakery was one of the first "new wave" of bakeries in Victoria that used a brick wood burning oven to bake all of their breads, and they've been going strong since 1998. Erika Heyrman and her then-husband Cliff Leir—now of Fol Epi—were the original owners, and some of the first proponents of trying to bring Red Fife wheat back into common use in Canada. Erika has carried on with the ownership of Wild Fire for over twenty-five years now, and during that time she opened the Nootka Rose milling operation in Metchosin. As much as possible, the grains used at Wild Fire are grown on Vancouver Island, and all grains for Wild Fire are milled at Nootka Rose to ensure their freshness. Wild Fire has maintained that "good old-fashioned" feel to its interior, and the brightly painted exterior means you can find it even during a Victorian thick fog. Picking up some bread or some of their awesome cookies there every so often feels a bit like stepping into a wholesome past . . . something we could use a lot more of these days. If you can't make it downtown, check their website to find their retail partners.

Erika Heyrman.

Working Culture Bread

2506 Douglas Street, Victoria | 250-388-7774
workingculturebread.com | IG: workingculturebread

Working Culture Bread lies just on the edge of downtown Victoria at the busy intersection of Douglas and Bay Streets. Easy to drive by on your first visit, but after that first visit, you'll never forget how to find it. First, there's the aroma of all good things like bread and pastry. Unforgettable. Then there is the actual flavour of it, especially the bread. When Jess Rivers and Adam Christie decided they wanted to open a bakery, the main reason was that they felt they couldn't find the kind of bread they were craving. Jess says, "Working Culture Bread has a deeply caramelized and flavourful exterior, and a custardy, chewy interior because of a very high-hydration dough. We eat bread daily, and our son is now a huge fan too. We feel good about feeding our family and the community this bread, which only contains flour, water, salt, and naturally fermented sourdough starter." So how did they become bakery owners in the first place? I love these backstories. Adam and Jess both came from corporate backgrounds, Adam in environmental science and Jess in the film and advertising industry. They met in Vancouver while both were working for LUSH cosmetics. But they soon realized they both had the same dream (or more like a fantasy) of opening a bakery. They took the plunge, quit their jobs, moved to Victoria, and started the process of becoming an important part of their neighbourhood, first with just themselves making and serving bread and coffee, and now with a wide variety of sweet and savoury pastries, sandwiches, and many different organic sourdough breads and plenty of help both behind and at the counter. Apparently, the cinnamon buns have developed quite a cult following!

○ **Adam Christie with his son Otto.**

Macaloney's Island Distillery

761 Enterprise Crescent, Saanich | 778-401-0410
macaloneydistillers.com | FB: Macaloney's Island Distillery

Dr. Graeme Macaloney.

When I interviewed Dr. Graeme Macaloney of Macaloney's Island Distillery for a CBC Radio feature, we talked in a little office outside the distillery, but the first thing I noticed in the office was that it was loaded with the distinct aroma of whiskey, but not a drop in sight. I mentioned that to Graeme, and he opened a door which I thought was a closet but led to a barrel room crammed with barrels of whiskey which he said were his special projects. That's when he told me that he had been taken with the whole idea of making whiskey since he was a boy. "I mean I started working in a whiskey factory (back home in Scotland) when I was a teenager, and that got me into studying fermentation." Eventually he earned a doctorate in fermentation and thought that was his ticket into a dream job at a distillery, only to be told he was overqualified. So he started working in fermentation and biotech, and that led him to Canada, where he developed his plan to open his own distillery, and Victoria was where he ended up. Some of his whiskeys started winning awards both in Canada and abroad, and success has garnered the attention—and the wrath—of the Scottish Whiskey Association. The SWA told him he couldn't use his own name on his whiskey brand or names like Glen Loy and Invermallie—places from his family's long history in Scotland. Even *Island* was problematic. After a strenuous social media campaign was launched to back Macaloney's, and a series of back-and-forth negotiations with the SWA, a compromise was reached, and yes, he could name the distillery after his family name and say it was on an island because it *is* on an island! The Macaloney team continues to create some fine whiskies, and the staff gives excellent tours of both the distillery and the Twa Dogs brewery contained in the same building. The beer brewing process is also one of the first steps in making whiskey. It's all fermentation, right?

Phillips Soda Works*

2010 Government Street, Victoria | 250-380-1912
phillipssoda.com | IG: phillipssoda

Sparkmouth Ginger Ale and Captain Electro's Intergalactic Root Beer were the first two products coming out of this 2012 subsidiary of Phillips Brewing. I get only an occasional craving for root beer, but I must toast Captain Electro for his Intergalactic Root Beer. It tastes smooth and rich, not at all harsh like more commercially produced sodas. The Sparkmouth Ginger Ale has a very zingy, upfront ginger flavour. New additions to the line include Speed King Craft Cola and Dare Devil Orange Cream. All feature cane sugar instead of high fructose corn syrup and real ingredients like ginger, licorice root, cloves, fruit juice, and real vanilla. The Orange Cream tastes just like the Cream Soda of my misspent youth, but not as sweet (yay!)

Phillips Brewing and Malting Company, founded by Matt Phillips in 2001, is best known for its beers, but is also a distillery and malting facility. I'm focusing on the sodas here because I love a quality local alternative to commercially made sodas.

Sheringham Distillery

103–4382 West Shore Parkway, Langford | 778-425-2019
sheringhamdistillery.com | IG: sheringhamdistillery

Alayne and Jason MacIsaac in the Sheringham Distillery tasting room.

British Columbia is rich with historic place names, some of which have faded away because the towns simply don't exist any longer. It happens a lot in a resource-rich (and then poor) economy. In the case of Sheringham, originally named after a British Navy commander in 1846, it was an economy of letters that led to a name change in 1893 when the post office came to Sheringham. Sheringham was shortened somehow to *Shirley* so the name could fit on a postage stamp. Why the history lesson? Sheringham and Shirley and the schooner *Favorite*—which plied the waters of nearby Juan de Fuca Strait and the Sheringham Lighthouse—are all part of the legacy of Sheringham Distillery, founded in Shirley in 2015 by husband-and-wife team Jason and Alayne MacIsaac. Since then, the distillery has gone through four major upgrades and moved to Sooke and then Langford. Their flagship gin, Seaside, uses sustainably harvested winged kelp as one of the botanicals used for flavouring. It won World's Best Contemporary Gin at the World Gin Awards in 2019. I'm especially fond of Sheringham's Rhubarb Gin Liqueur, which packs a lighter punch on the alcohol percentage but presents a great rhubarb flavour augmented by star anise and lemon peel. Back to the history lesson. Every bottle of Sheringham product—which also includes whiskey, vodka, and other liqueurs—is embossed with an emblem of the schooner *Favorite*, and the bottle is a similar shape to some old Prohibition-era moonshine bottles Jason came across near the site of an old still.

Spinnakers Gastro Brewpub

308 Catherine Street, Victoria | 250-386-2739
spinnakers.com | IG: spinnakersbrewpub

I have a penchant for things that are vinegary in nature. At any given time, you will find at least half a dozen different types of vinegar in a tall drawer in my kitchen. One of those vinegars is always a malt vinegar from Spinnakers Gastro Brewpub. Of course, Spinnakers is well known for its beer and was Canada's very first brewpub, ushering in the new age of craft beer when it opened in 1984. Now the company has expanded into ciders as well as spirits like vodka and gin. But some of the beers brewed in their stainless-steel tanks are encouraged to turn to vinegar and then are placed in oak barrels to carefully age for several months in the craft tradition. Commercial vinegars are merely acetic acid with some caramel colouring added to give the appearance of an aged vinegar, but they taste sharp and crude. Why buy that when you can get the real stuff? Now, it may be that you have visited Spinnakers just to get some vinegar, but I recommend trying the Cask of the Day at the bar, maybe some BC mussels steamed in ale from the menu, and a lengthy browse at the Spinnakers provisions store near the entrance to the pub. There you will find a wide selection of vinegars, along with house-made, beer-based mustards, breads, baked goods and pastries, other beer-based condiments, and even chocolate truffles, as well as items from other artisans mentioned in this book, such as the Vancouver Island Salt Company and Salt Spring Island Cheese. Spinnakers is now also making sodas, sparkling mineral waters, and premium mixers. And if you stay for a meal in the pub, you will be rewarded with one of the best oceanfront dining views in the city.

Farm + Field Butchers

1003 Blanshard Street, Victoria | 250-415-8373
farmandfieldbutchers.com | IG: farmandfieldbutchers

Rebecca Teskey.

When I first met Rebecca Teskey it was back in the early 2010s when she was part-owner of the Village Butcher in Oak Bay. At that time, and I think even today, it's unusual to find a woman adeptly wielding a knife in a butcher shop, let alone being the owner. Like many other top jobs in the culinary world, they are still in the male domain. Rebecca changed that when she sold her share in the Village Butcher and opened Farm + Field Butchers in downtown Victoria in 2016. Since then, she's continued to build her reputation on practising whole-animal butchery with meats and poultry she sources from quality farms in the area. Using the whole animal means she and her team can create many more products, less waste, and more selection for her customers. Rebecca is quick to credit part of her success to skilled employees who have stuck around for the long haul. Experienced butchers are hard to find, so keeping them around is important. Along with the full-service meat counter, the front of the shop stocks a great variety of food items to help make your cooking and entertaining easier. Tinned fish are all the rage these days, and you'll find the best sardines, anchovies, and mackerel in beautiful packaging there, along with specialty products brought in from Victoria's Fol Epi Bakery and smoked meat products from Four Quarters Meats. The downtown crowd can tend to be more of an on-the-go type, so there are plenty of marinated selections, chicken soup, burgers, already-cooked chicken wings, and so on.

Galloping Goose Sausage Company

4484 Lindholm Road, Metchosin | 250-474-5788

info@gallopinggoosesausage.com | gallopinggoosesausage.com

The Galloping Goose Sausage Company of Metchosin has been around since 1994, when it became the full-time jobs of Johan Wessels and Kate Wallace. Johan was the instigator. An immigrant from South Africa, he was missing the processed meat products of his homeland and figured he could just recreate them here without really knowing much about how to make fresh and dried sausages. Their backgrounds were graphics and engineering. Luckily, he had some help come along in the form of a Polish sausage maker named Kaz Jachowicz, who was supposed to be retired but worked with the company until he was seventy-four. The first sausage Johan made, even before Kaz came on the scene, was boerewors, a kind of the national sausage of South Africa. Johan and Kate visited friends in South Africa and came back with enough knowledge to make a good go of the boerewors. Friends liked it so much they kept making more and more and so the company was born. They still make boerewors and two other South African specialties—droewors, which is boerewors dried to an intensely flavoured chewy texture, and biltong, which is an allspice and coriander marinated type of jerky. From there they expanded their line of offerings to include many different varieties of gluten-free sausages made from pork, beef, chicken, and even bison. They use meats from locally and ethically raised animals produced without antibiotics and growth hormones. Phone ahead to pick up sausages at their production facility and consult their website for retail locations. The time has come for Johan and Kate to step aside from the day to day running of the company and pass things on to the next generations as seen in the photo.

Left to right: Johan, Duncan, Sammi, Alexis, and Annalise Wessels, and Kate Wallace.

Haus Sausage Co.

4–515 Dupplin Road, Victoria | 778-433-4287
haussausageco.com | IG: haussausageco

Kyle Clayton and Shane Harwood.

Shane Harwood and Kyle Clayton founded Haus Sausage Co. in 2017 with a desire to start their own business after working various jobs in the hospitality and restaurant industry, notably with Cory Pelan and The Whole Beast Artisan Salumeria and Village Butcher. Like many food artisans, they started small by taking their products to a single farmers' market. You can still find them at the year-round markets like Moss Street Market in Victoria and the Duncan Farmers' Market, and seasonally at the Esquimalt and Metchosin markets. But they have their own shop in Victoria open four days a week and distribute their products to restaurants and retailers around the island and even a few in the Lower Mainland.

They aren't afraid to experiment with their flavours, and that's what makes them stand out from some of the other sausage makers. I love their maple blueberry sausages and chorizo verde, and they continue to expand their repertoire into bags of beef barbacoa and chicken tinga that just need to be reheated, and they can even put together individual-sized charcuterie boards. Along with the chorizo verde, their most popular products are their dry pepperoni and biltong beef jerky, which have proven to be much more successful than they ever expected. Best thing about their jobs? "Our customers are the best. Most have been with us for years."

McLennan's Island Meat and Seafood

307 Cook Street, Victoria | 250-382-3331
mclennansislandmeatandseafood.com | IG: islandmeatandseafood

Lloyd McLennan.

Lloyd McLennan is a ferocious promoter of local meats, poultry, and seafood. Maybe that's why his nickname is the Meatdogg. His packed shop is full of fresh and marinated meats and seafood and local processed food products. With butchery in his roots, Lloyd believes in preparing products for his customers "just as I would like it for myself" and makes sure all his staff share his knowledge of the provenance of their products. During my visit, as we walked along his meat counter, he pointed out Tannadice Farms pork, "but I'm also getting a lot of beef from them, chicken from Island Farmhouse Poultry. The lamb is local as well from Parry Bay Farm in Metchosin." He does admit to bringing in some beef from Alberta, but it's from a rancher he knows, and there's no other way to keep the higher-end cuts like tenderloins and rib-eyes in stock. Lloyd also makes a great variety of hamburgers and sausages and will do custom work at the drop of a hat. "If a customer happens to be allergic to garlic, I'll make up sausages just for them without garlic or any other ingredient they don't like or can't handle."

The Whole Beast Artisan Salumeria and Village Butcher

2032 Oak Bay Avenue, Victoria

THE WHOLE BEAST

250-590-7675 (PORK) | thewholebeast.ca | IG: wholebeastmeats

I first met co-owner Cory Pelan of the Whole Beast and Village Butcher when he was the chef at an Italian restaurant in Victoria. His contract there was about to end, and he was thinking about moving to another restaurant. Then he had second thoughts. "I kind of had an epiphany with a pig one afternoon. I was in the kitchen, working with a whole carcass, breaking it down and eventually making maybe fifteen or twenty different products with it, and thinking that this was the happiest I'd been in my working life, so that's when I thought I could do something like this full-time." When some retail and prep space became available beside Village Butcher in Oak Bay Village, he was ready to make the leap from chef to salumist. My favourites are any number of the dry-cured sausages he makes, including the pork sausage laced with fennel seeds or the spicy chorizo castellano. Some former employees and partners of Cory both on the salumi and butchery side have gone on the create their own respected companies, like Geoff Pinch of Four Quarters Meats and Shane Harwood and Kyle Clayton of Haus Sausage Co.

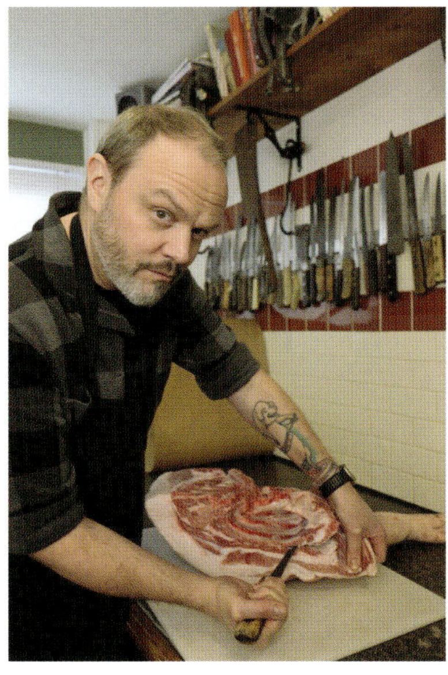

Cory Pelan working on a whole leg of pork.

VILLAGE BUTCHER

250-598-1115 | villagebutcher.ca | IG: therealvillagebutcher

There isn't even a wall between the retail space of The Whole Beast Artisan Salumeria and Village Butcher. Convenient, that is. While the Whole Beast specializes in curing meats, Village Butcher is your place next door for fresh meats and fresh sausages, and a growing selection of take-home offerings like soups, stews, lasagne, pot pies, and meat loaf. You need pure lard, or duck fat? They have that, too, along with house-made marinades, spice rubs, and stocks. Cory and co-owner Michael Windle source most of their pork from one farmer in Metchosin. Other individual farms are the main providers of lamb, chicken, and beef, with the farthest farm being in Comox. You are definitely eating the finest the island has to offer. You'll pay a little more for your meats here, but once you've tried their chimichurri flank steak grilled and thinly sliced, you will know that it's worth it.

YOU MIGHT ALSO WANT TO TRY:

- **Glenwood Meats**, 1245 Parkdale Drive, Langford (250-478-6328). Founded in 1950, Glenwood Meats boasts a full-service meat counter.

- **Slaters Meats**, 2577 Cadboro Bay Road, Oak Bay (250-592-0823). Founded in 1954, Slaters Meats has built a loyal following over the generations.

The Chocolate Project

1311 Blanshard Street, Victoria | 250-595-8466
chocolateproject.ca | IG: thechocpro

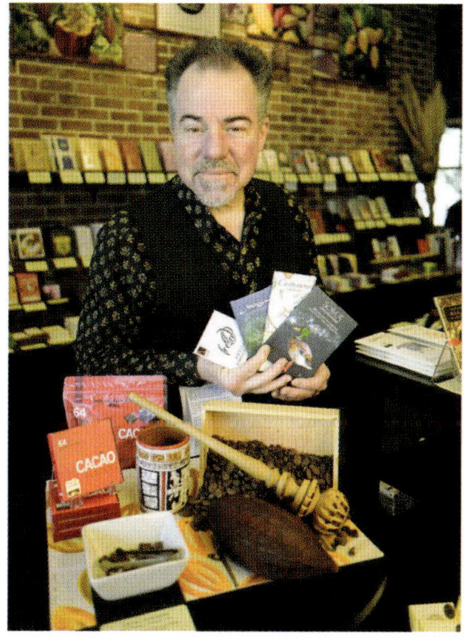

David Mincey.

David Mincey made his appearance in the first edition of this book as a chef and the co-founder of the Island Chefs Collaborative, on a mission to put together restaurant chefs and farmers to mutual benefit. I mentioned he was also interested in sourcing high-quality bean-to-bar fair trade chocolate from all over the world. He would then distribute those products to small retailers all over Victoria. Back then, he boasted of about 180 different bars from a few dozen manufacturers. Fast forward a decade, and he has opened his own retail shop and chocolate education centre in the Atrium Building in downtown Victoria. Now he rotates through 350 different chocolate bars coming from 65 different countries. The shop is beautiful as, over the years, chocolate packaging has become inventive, bright, and colourful. Yes, there are always samples. And if you're into locally produced bean-to-bar delights, David is proud to stock the products of four local companies—Sirene, Wallace, Black Jaguar, and Uncouth Chocolate, which was founded by two of David's former chocolate concierges at the shop. He's happy to work with new people venturing into the world of bean-to-bar chocolate, but when I asked him if he ever wanted to go into chocolate making himself, he said that he had made chocolate in the past, but eventually had to decide whether he wanted to be a chocolate maker or have the time to taste and judge chocolate from around the world and educate people about a product that is just as or even more complex than other revered foods and beverages. Lucky for Victoria, he chose educator and retailer.

Rogers' Chocolates

Five Locations: 913 Government Street, Victoria | 4253 Commerce Circle, Victoria | 2234 Oak Bay Avenue, Victoria | Unit 129-3551, Uptown Boulevard, Victoria | 2423 Beacon Avenue, Sidney
250-384-7021 | rogerschocolates.com | FB: Rogers' Chocolates

This is really the granddaddy of all the chocolate-making businesses in British Columbia. It began over 125 years ago in the back of a grocery store in Victoria owned by Charles Rogers, who became known as "Candy" Rogers when his sweets became popular. One year, close to Christmas, I was invited to tour the Rogers' Chocolates factory not far from downtown Victoria. After I put on my lab coat and hairnet, I was literally a kid in a candy factory as I was shown around by their master chocolatier. The aroma just surrounds you, and I think I was floating off the floor just from that. You can't believe what it's like to see giant slabs of chocolate and vats of melting chocolate and little nougats heading down a conveyor belt to be drenched in more chocolate! While the company has historic roots, Rogers' is constantly inventing new products to satisfy the cravings of chocoholics, including a line of organic chocolate bars and—my favourite—pink and white sea salt-topped vanilla caramels. Part of Rogers's strength is that not only does it make good-tasting chocolate, but it also puts those products in wonderful packaging, often featuring local artists, for a true keepsake.

Charles "Candy" Rogers and wife Leah.

Sirene Chocolate

Victoria | sirenechocolate.com | IG: sirenechocolate

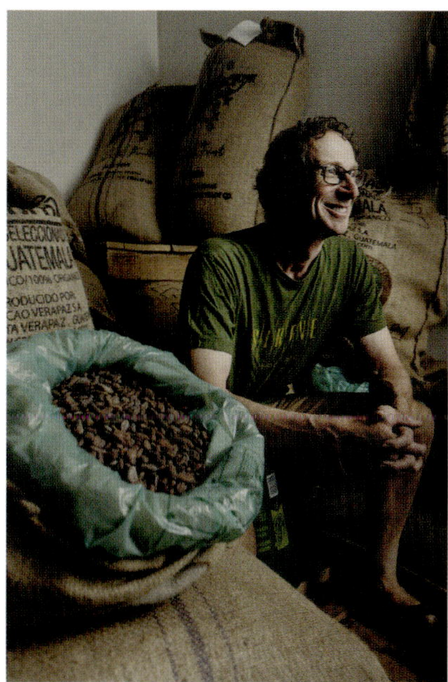

Taylor Kennedy.

Sirene is one of Victoria's best-known brands of bean-to-bar chocolate. When I say best-known, I mean best-known around the world. In addition to being available in shops across Canada and the US, Sirene pops up in France, the United Kingdom, and Australia. Since being founded in 2013 by Taylor Kennedy, Sirene has garnered multiple international awards for a company that has stayed fairly small and adhered to its philosophy of using high quality beans purchased directly from farmers who employ favourable working conditions. This puts two small businesses together, the farm and the chocolate maker to make the best chocolate possible for customers. I'm partial to the fleur de sel, a 73 percent dark chocolate made with cacao beans from Uganda and salt flakes from the Vancouver Island Salt Company. The beans for other bars come from many different countries and reflect Kennedy's roots as a world traveller when he was working in the photography department of *National Geographic*. If you're interested in a chocolate beverage instead of a chocolate bar, Sirene sends its husks and shells of cacao beans discarded in the chocolate making process to Sheringham Distillery, where Jason MacIsaac has created a Sirene Chocolate Liqueur.

Wallace Craft Chocolate

Victoria | wallacechocolate.com | IG: wallacecraftchocolate

Mark Wallace.

Out of Africa. That's the phrase that comes to mind when I think of Wallace Craft Chocolate because that is where the company's origins lie. Before it sprang into being a few years ago, Mark Wallace had been working in fine cocoa and sustainability within the cocoa sector in West Africa for five years before returning to Victoria. For a dozen years his involvement in supporting businesses, responsible supply chains, and sustainability initiatives took him to many countries on the African continent working with agricultural products. But Liberia found him focused on a project supporting the cocoa sector, which needed rebuilding in a post-conflict era with many factors to consider, including the quality and yield of the cacao trees, and critical child labour, gender, and environmental components. While working on all of that and working to get better prices for the farmers, Mark was able to interact with professionals within the Cocoa of Excellence program and master chocolatiers in France, Belgium, and the Netherlands. Nothing like learning from the best! Now Mark says the company has grown from experimenting on a kitchen counter with cocoa beans that he brought back from Liberia to making chocolate that has won awards and a gold medal at the international chocolate awards. All of their beans are 100 percent transparently traded—which is a step up from fair trade or organic certifications, and they work with farmers to make the very best cocoa. The products they're proudest of include the Liberia 81 percent dark bar and 45 percent milk bar. "They are close to my heart," says Mark. "I worked really hard with the farmers in Liberia so that they would produce cocoa beans of a quality high enough for fine chocolate makers. They are among our top sellers, too—our customers love them."

Mile Zero Coffee Company

101–2612 Bridge Street, Victoria | 778-265-1428
milezerocoffee.com | IG: milezerocoffeeco

I'm leading off the coffee section in this part of the book with Mile Zero Coffee Company as it is unique in its approach to roasting coffee here. Brad Scissons and business partner Derek Hughson use small air roasters instead of big drum roasters. An air roaster allows a greater balance of roasting to be formed in the beans because they are surrounded by hot air at all times as opposed to being dragged over the hot metal of the inside of a drum. They roast in small, twenty-pound batches of strictly organic first and second grade coffee beans. Brad explained to me you can get a much more earthy and full-bodied flavour out of roasting the beans a little longer, and a dark roast doesn't have to be bitter. I usually need to have milk in my coffee, but in tasting one of Brad's darker roasts I could easily drink it black with nothing added. Brad worked in the hospitality industry before he came to coffee roasting, and his contacts within that industry have helped him forge ties with dozens of commercial accounts with restaurants and hotels and a smattering of small retailers in the Greater Victoria area. Mile Zero got its start in 2009 at the now-defunct Niagara Grocery store in James Bay with two small air roasters, which is where Brad learned how to roast coffee until he and Derek eventually bought the brand. Up until Mile Zero

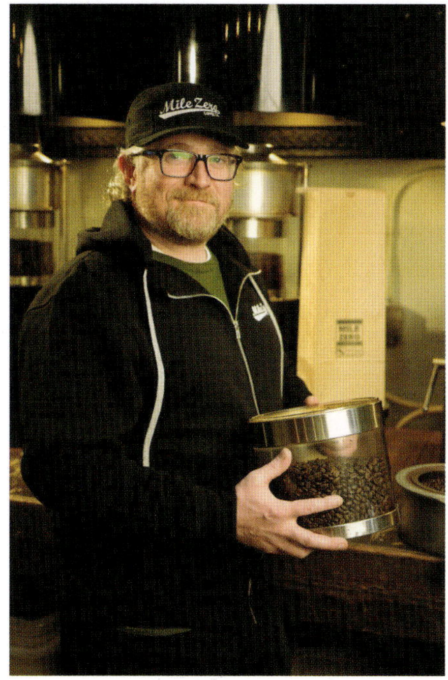

Brad Scissons with his air roasters.

Mile Zero Coffee Company

moved into its new facility in Rock Bay in 2020, beans were being roasted in a little shack on the Devine Vineyards property in Saanichton, and they were even roasting beans in propane-fired air roasters at the Moss Street Market. Brad says the aroma was heavenly on those market mornings and a great way to attract market-goers to their stall so they could explain the different process. And his connection with the DEVINE Distillery meant access to some barrels that had been used to age spirits such as whiskey that had been made with grains grown on the island. He now stuffs the barrels with green coffee beans so they can absorb some flavour from the whiskey barrels before roasting for a very heady aroma in the final product.

OTHER QUALITY ROASTERS WITH CAFÉS IN THE GREATER VICTORIA AREA:

- **Fernwood Coffee**, including the Parsonage (fernwoodcoffee.com)
- **Discovery Coffee**, five locations (discoverycoffee.com)
- **Habit Coffee**, two locations, featuring roasting partner Bows Coffee (habitcoffee.com)
- **2% Jazz Coffee**, four locations (2percentjazz.com)

Murchie's Tea & Coffee

1110 Government Street, Victoria | 250-383-3112
murchies.com | IG: murchiestea

I'm including Murchie's in this group as an Island food artisan even though the company has several locations on the Lower Mainland and its head office is in Richmond. I think you can really call the Murchie's in the Alhambra building on Government Street the flagship store. It looks as if it has been a permanent fixture in Victoria, although the 1907 building was renovated in 1986, and the ground floor became the new home to Murchie's. The company goes back to 1894 when John Murchie came from Scotland to New Westminster to found Murchie's Tea & Coffee. Now the company specializes in over a hundred different blends of fair-trade teas and coffees, but the real treat is walking in the front door on the café side of the store and struggling to decide which of the array of pastries and sweets to choose from to go with your tea or coffee. I'm quite content with a pot of Earl Grey and a currant scone and clotted cream, carried to my table on a fancy metal tray. Makes me feel like I am an honorary member of the British Empire, if just for a few minutes in the afternoon—and it's much cheaper than afternoon tea at the Fairmont Empress!

The "Wall of Tea" at Murchie's.

Silk Road Tea

1624 Government Street, Victoria | 250-388-6815
silkroadteastore.com | IG: silkroadtea

Daniela Cubelic founded Silk Road Tea in 1992, and since then she's been a genuine ambassador of tea to thousands of contented sippers. Whenever I speak with her, I learn new things about tea—what's in it, the health benefits, the flavour profiles, what shouldn't be in it, and so on. Her enthusiasm for all things tea is mirrored in her staff, who are always ready with help or advice. Silk Road always has some sort of tea ready for you to try when you walk in the door, although there isn't always a door, and sometimes you will find Daniela or some of her employees at a food festival, doling out free samples that were carefully chosen for the occasion. The store on Government Street is an oasis of calm, featuring beautiful merchandising of all of the products on offer. While Daniela's an expert in the history of tea and its traditions, she also has a keen interest in taking tea beyond tradition by cooking with tea, developing tea cocktails and tea and food pairings. She has even incorporated tea in Silk Road's skin and body care products. On her agenda these days is carefully monitoring climate change and its effect on the production of tea around the world.

Daniela Cubelic.

Leechtown Blacksmith Co.

Sooke | leechtown.co | IG: leechtownblacksmithco

Good kitchen gear isn't cheap. But if you put out the money, Ryan Fogarty guarantees each frypan, knife, or cutlery set you buy from him instantly becomes an heirloom piece worthy of mentioning in your will. Ryan is the creative force behind Leechtown Blacksmith Co. in Sooke. Leechtown is now a ghost town, but in the 1860s, it was the site of a gold rush. Appropriate name for a company working with metal. Ryan grew up in Sooke but ended up working with his father in the steel trade in Alberta, doing everything from welding to teaching welding to being a welding inspector for around twenty years. During one Christmas holiday, he decided he didn't want to go back to his regular job because he wanted to become a blacksmith and started accumulating all the tools of the trade. He was working with a metal sculpture artist for a few years before deciding that, since he has always been a foodie, his metal art should be used in the kitchen. His Leechtown line now includes carbon steel knives, frying pans, and custom cutlery. His pieces are in places as far-flung as the Nimmo Bay Wilderness Resort across the strait from Port Hardy, and world-famous Noma Restaurant in Copenhagen, Denmark. Ryan is a firm believer in both the cooking qualities and healthy nature of cooking with carbon steel frying pans. They heat fast, cool down fast, and work on all kinds of stovetops. I liked the promotion he ran during Christmas of 2023 . . . bring in your old non-stick coated frying pans and he'd give you a rebate on one of his pans.

o **Ryan Fogarty.**

Penna & Co. Kitchen & Giftwares

777 Royal Oak Drive, Victoria | 250-727-2110
info@pennakitchen.com | pennakitchen.com | FB: Penna & Co.

Michelle Tindale (Penna).

Penna & Co. traces its history back to 1993, when Peter and Heidi Penna opened the cookware store in a fairly small shop in the Broadmead Village outdoor mall. It was supposed to be a retirement project for them, but over thirty years later the store has expanded, and the business has been passed on to the Penna daughters, Shalene and Michelle. It's my favourite kitchen shop in Victoria, and it has many other fans as well. There's always something new to look at, whether it's a new apron to add to my collection, a useful gadget that I will actually use on a regular basis, or something I can give to my niece to add to her growing collection of cookware as she gets more adventurous with her cooking. With such a broad spectrum of kitchen equipment and dining accessories, it's good to know that the staff there have been well-trained and are ready to help you out when you're lost or don't know exactly what you're looking for.

Russell Books

100–747 Fort Street, Victoria | 250-361-4447
russellbooks.com | IG: russellbooksvictoria

I have to admit a bias off the start of this listing. My wife, Ramona Montagnes, works part-time at Russell Books, and in the past, I used to do a cookbook feature for the store called Foodie Friday. Every week I would select a few cookbooks from the selection at the store, cook some of the dishes, take photos, and put together a video demonstrating why I liked those particular cookbooks. There. But here are the facts: Russell Books has the largest collection of cookbooks for sale in the city, probably in the whole province. There are thousands of food-related books to browse there—new, used, and *new remaindered*, which is to say books that have never been sold before but were excess to the publisher's needs and deep discounted and are now are available to you at very good prices. But it's not just cookbooks on every imaginable subject. It's books on beer and wine and special diets; it's food literature and travel and food memoirs from chefs and food writers. Russell Books is the largest used bookstore in Canada, and the food and cooking section is second only in size to the fiction section of the store. Can't find the book you're looking for? They'll take your name and get in touch when it comes in . . . even if it's years later! Can't get to the city? They do online sales and will ship you the books. Russell Books was started by Reg Russell in Montreal in 1961 and opened operations in Victoria in 1991. Today, Reg's granddaughter Andrea Minter and her husband Jordan Minter manage the store, and I'm glad they love cookbooks as much as I do.

Andrea and Jordan Minter.

The Tuscan Kitchen

653 View Street, Victoria | 250-386-8191
thetuscankitchen.com | IG: the.tuscan.kitchen

Gerri and Mauro Schelini.

Mauro Schelini and his wife, Gerri, have put together a wonderful collection of Italian pottery in their European-themed shop, which nearly makes me cry when I walk in because it reminds me I don't get to Italy as often as I would like! Majolica pottery from different Italian manufacturers is the main attraction here, but the Tuscan Kitchen also retails top European brands of knives and cookware and a pantry full of imported foodstuffs like high-quality extra-virgin olive oil and dried pastas. If you're into making linguine from scratch, they will be happy to sell you a pasta machine as well. Where they really shine is in the tableware and especially linens imported from Italy that are just gorgeous. I'm not usually into linens, but I have to say what they carry is just so impressive and modern-looking and not the stuff like your Italian grandmother used to cover in plastic. (My Italian aunts were like my grandmothers, and they always had plastic over the crocheted tablecloths on the dining room table.)

YOU MIGHT ALSO WANT TO TRY:

Paboom Home Imports, 1437 Store Street, Victoria (250-380-0020). You never know what you'll find in this shop, but chances are there will be something you can use in your kitchen, like Weck jars, gorgeous resin bowls, or even soap made from beer.

Whisk, 1702 Douglas Street, Victoria (778-433-9184). Whisk is tucked into one end of Victoria Public Market and offers an incredible array of cookware, kitchen tools, linens, aprons, and much more very artfully arranged in what is quite a tiny space. Check here for wide selections of Rosti bowls and Le Creuset cookware you don't often find in larger shops.

Cold Comfort Ice Cream Company

2–1115 North Park Street, Victoria | 778-432-2653
coldcomfort.ca | IG: coldcomforticecreamcompany

If you've ever stopped to read the label on a commercially produced carton of ice cream, you may have put down your spoon and reached for a dictionary or perhaps gone to the internet to figure out what all the ingredients are. Not so with Autumn Maxwell's Cold Comfort Ice Cream. She makes every small batch the old-fashioned way, with organic cream, milk, eggs, and cane sugar, and even a touch of salt from Vancouver Island Salt Company. Those ingredients make for a good ice cream right there, but Autumn takes it one step further by offering unheard-of, yet alluring, combinations in a never-ending swirl of creativity. In this book's first edition, she had created over two hundred separate concoctions. As I write this edition, ten years later, she's up to over four hundred. I warn you that some of her flavours may not be available at all times, or maybe ever again—it's all up to Autumn. One of my all-time favourites? Sour cherry and rosemary. It's now called Rosemary's Baby. She sells her concoctions in pints but also puts together fantastic combinations with baked goods acting as the bread in a sandwich. So you might get maple-syrup ice cream surrounded by walnut-vanilla meringue cookies, or graham-crumb cookies stuffed with strawberry-cheesecake ice cream. There doesn't seem to be a limit to her imagination. She moved into offering some popular vegan and gluten free products (NiceCream) using a coconut milk base. In 2024, she celebrated ten years at what she calls Cold Comfort HQ, her manufacturing and storefront facility in Victoria's North Park neighbourhood, just off Cook Street, and a total of fourteen years in business. Her products are sold in a number of independent retailers in and around Victoria. It

Autumn Maxwell in her s-Cargo ice cream truck.

» Cold Comfort Ice Cream Company

hasn't been an easy road. Just sourcing enough organic cream to put into her products sometimes proved to be difficult. And then after carefully observing Canadian Food Inspection Agency labelling requirements so she could wholesale her product to retailers, the Island Health authority told her she either had to become a Licensed Dairy Plant (very costly and complicated) or use a pre-made organic cream base in her dairy-based products. But you can't get that kind of base on Vancouver Island, and Autumn would never resort to that kind of product anyway. So now you can only get her dairy-based products at Cold Comfort HQ in North Park while her retail connections still sell the non-dairy NiceCreams.

Parachute Ice Cream

105–2626 Bridge Street, Victoria | 778-265-1999
129–735 Goldstream Avenue, Langford | 250-419-8390
parachuteicecream.com | IG: parachuteicecream

It's pretty good when something you considered just as a hobby to start with turns into a thriving business with two locations. It helps that the hobby was making ice cream, and as Parachute Ice Cream co-owner Kevin Fung says, "It makes people happy. It's not like the dentist, people come to treat themselves and bring a smile to their lips." Fung and his fellow ice cream hobbyist Robyn Larocque opened as a small hobby shop in Victoria's Rock Bay neighbourhood in 2016. They thought high quality accessible ice cream was missing from Victoria and thought it would be fun to bring it to their family, friends, and a small audience of locals. Fast forward to now and they have doubled their production space and opened a second outlet in Langford in 2021 where you can now get take-home pies from the Victoria Pie Company (pie and ice cream, get it?). The ice cream they make and sell in returnable glass jars is a combination of richer and heavier North American ingredients paired with traditional Italian gelato production methods. They try to use as many local products as they can. This includes water buffalo milk from McClintock's Farm in the Comox Valley, Babe's Honey, kiwi fruit from the Saanich Peninsula, and many more. The hardest thing about selling a product people usually love? "The seasonal fluctuation of business," says Kevin. "The most fun, but most challenging part really, is constantly innovating new flavour concepts after the hundreds we've already made."

Parachute Team Leader Kayleah Diehl.

Dakini Tidal Wilds

Victoria | 250-818-4633 | dakinitidalwilds.com | IG: dakinitidalwilds

Amanda Swinimer showing some seaweed found when the tide was out in Sooke.

Amanda Swinimer's passion is kelp. Yes, that green stuff from the sea. Around thirty different kinds of kelp are found in the waters around Vancouver Island. It's easy to get caught up in her passion if you listen to her talk about the medicinal and nutritional qualities of this seaweed she's been harvesting on a commercial basis since the early 2000s. Her sustainably harvested products include dried winged kelp and bull kelp, rich in minerals and vitamins. Her dried product is available online. Her Mermaid's Shake is great on popcorn! Chefs also order seaweed from her to use on their menus. Seaweed is loaded with umami, that mysterious fifth basic taste after sweet, salty, sour, and bitter that may be hard to describe other than saying, "tastes good." Amanda got turned onto seaweed while learning about wild crafting with herbs. "You should have seen my tiny one-bedroom apartment," she laughs. "It was always laced wall-to-wall with long strings of seaweed hanging to dry." Dakini is a goddess found in Indian beliefs, among others. Amanda's favourite definition of Dakini fits her to a T: "the wild and free-dancing spirit of women."

Jenny Marie's Cracker Company

2740 Rock Bay Avenue, Unit A, Victoria | info@jennymariescrackers.com
jennymariescrackers.com | IG: jennymariescrackers

Jenny Marie.

Having once owned and operated a small food business company myself, I can appreciate all the hard work that goes into creating a product that you first make at home with little or no equipment to make it easier, then selling your products first at farmers' markets and hoping you can get your big break by selling to retailers. This is the route that Jenny Marie took with her vegan cracker company. Except at first it wasn't a cracker company. Jenny grew up in St. John's, Newfoundland, with two grandmothers who instilled in her not only a love of baking but the importance of using quality ingredients to make good food. After moving to Victoria, she felt the urge to create something in an entrepreneurial fashion, and her husband suggested putting her love of baking to work and try selling it at the weekly James Bay Market. Along with the crackers she was also baking cupcakes and muffins. Her audience at the market spoke: they loved the crackers most. That was in 2011, and by 2012, Jenny had dropped the other baked goods and was selling to retail shops in Victoria. At this point she was still mixing the dough by hand and rolling it thin with a rolling pin before topping with some ingredients, cutting by hand, baking, and packaging. Labour intensive! Now she has four people working for her in a commercial facility in Rock Bay with a big mixer for the dough and a commercial dough sheeter to roll it out. The toppings, cutting, baking, and packaging are all still done by hand. Her most popular sellers are Thyme & Sea Salt, Pepper & Sea Salt, and Simply Sea Salt. Jenny's personal favourite is the Thyme & Sea Salt because it was the first flavour she brought to the market when she started out fourteen years ago.

MAiiZ Nixtamal Eatery & Tortilleria

540 Fisgard Street, Victoria | 778-433-1544 | maiiz.ca | IG: maiiz.nixtamal

I consider myself somewhat lucky in life because I've had the opportunity to experience several *a-ha* moments over the years when I say to myself, "Oh, so *that's* what it's supposed to taste like." Ranking right up there is my first taste of a tortilla made with nixtamalized corn developed by Chef Israel Alvarez Molina of MAiiZ Nixtamal. Chef Israel moved to Canada in 2008 and almost immediately discovered he was missing a vital part of his traditional Mexican cuisine, nixtamalized corn, a process that takes dried corn kernels, brines them, and grinds them. When I tried my first MAiiZ tortilla I had that *a-ha* moment. There was so much more flavour to the tortilla, and I love the texture, too, a little coarser than a flour or regular corn tortilla, which makes for a more toothsome bite when you add your taco fillings. Slowly the word spread about these tortillas made with this special corn (made with organic BC corn kernels), and now it is possible to find MAiiZ tortillas in many independent and chain grocery stores on south Vancouver Island. You can also visit the MAiiZ Tortilleria & Eatery in Victoria's Chinatown. You can watch the tortillas coming off the pressing and cooking line, or buy the fresh dough if you want to make them yourself, and find products like the MAiiZ traditional black mole, salsas, and tortilla chips. The eatery offers tacos, quesadillas, tamales, chilaquiles, pozole soup, and more.

Israel Alvarez Molina.

Saltwest Naturals

Sooke | 778-977-3994 | saltwest.ca | IG: saltwest

Saltwest Naturals is just one of the salt companies that sprang up after Vancouver Island Sea Salt proved there was a market for" "home-grown" sea salt. Jeff and Jessica Abel harvest their ocean water near Sooke and use both a reverse osmosis process and boilers to produce their salt crystals. Since they started operation in 2011, the Abels have expanded their product line of edible salts to bath soaks and use the by-products of their salt production in ocean mineral soaps. In the early days, much of their time was spent selling direct to customers at farmers' markets, but now their products are available in more than three hundred locations across Canada. I'm a fan of their Raincoast Flor de Sal with its delicate flakes and another bestseller is the Salted Caramel Chocolate Sea Salt, one that Jessica is especially proud of. "I wanted it to be completely natural," she says, "so figuring out how to recreate that caramel chocolatey taste without using synthetic natural flavours was a challenge. But I kept working on it until my friends insisted I had it figured out." I love their origin story, as told by Jessica. "I was looking for a new career, and really felt passionate about the lack of local food options we had on Vancouver Island. My husband kept bugging me for a new boat, so he pitched the idea that I could start a business making Canadian sea salt, and if he had a bigger boat, he could get me loads of seawater when he went fishing. I was hooked, but the joke was on him 'cause we got so busy making salt there wasn't much time left for fishing anymore."

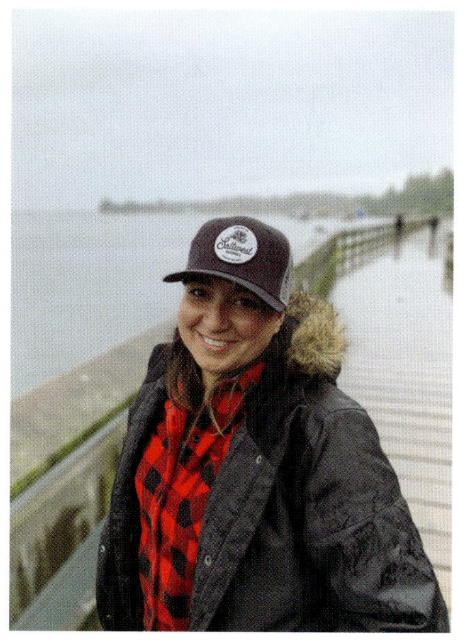

Jessica Abel, close to the source of her sea salt.

Finest at Sea Seafood Market and Food Truck

27 Erie Street, Victoria | 250-383-7760
finestatsea.com | FB: Finest at Sea Victoria

Bob Fraumeni, the founder of Finest at Sea, bought his first fishing boat in 1977 and hasn't looked back, expanding the fleet to ten large offshore fishing vessels and opening a retail shop in Victoria right across from Fisherman's Wharf Park. The name of Bob's company in 1984 was Frozen at Sea Seafood Producers, or FAS. He knew back then the importance of being able to deliver a quality product, whether it was fresh or frozen. Fish caught far from port may languish for days, or even more than a week, in the hold of a boat, its freshness and firm texture deteriorating by the minute. The FAS catch goes into a −60 °F freezer as soon as possible after being caught, and that frozen product is often much better quality than anything that gets to the consumer labelled as *fresh*. Years ago I asked Bob to speak at a food-culture class I was teaching at the University of Victoria, and for a short presentation, he insisted on bringing in a bunch of toaster ovens to heat up some smoked sablefish for the class, showed a video of the wild sea conditions he and his crew endure to catch that sablefish, and struggled to keep his temper under control while he listened to a spokesperson from the farmed-salmon industry give his spiel to my students. Fortunately, the only fuse blown was the one attached to a toaster oven, and I knew I had met someone who cares deeply about providing a quality wild, sustainable product to his customers. Bob still goes out salmon fishing each summer on the *Scania Queen* while mentoring future fishers. Finest at Sea also has a food truck right by the seafood shop where you can get fish and chips, chowder, seafood burgers, and tacos.

Bob Fraumeni with one of his boats at Fisherman's Wharf.

Charelli's Cheese Shop and Delicatessen

2851 Foul Bay Road, Victoria | 250-598-4794
charellis.com | IG: charellischeese

I wasn't around in Victoria when Charelli's first opened in 2003, but I've been enough times since then to know that this shop always offers something different no matter how many times you go in. Yes, you can always count on there being cheese and meats and local and imported goods there, mostly of a European nature, but there's always a different cheese, a different condiment, a tool you never knew you needed until then, or a tub of Marcona almonds that instantly addicted you to their flat-shaped, salty/oily goodness. Imagine my pleasant surprise when our real estate agent sent us a gift basket full of goodies from Charelli's on the day we took possession of our house in Victoria! The place is well-known for its quality and service . . . and maybe a bit for the aisles that can get somewhat crowded with both products and people. But that's a good thing when you can rub elbows with other like-minded foodies and share your discoveries. If you like the shop and the people, you'll be happy to know Charelli's also does full-service catering. There is nobody named Charelli at the company, however. Deli founder Carmen Lassooij named it after a restaurant she visited in the Netherlands many years ago: "a place in the Netherlands that holds a lot of special memories and *gezellig* meaning cozy, quaint, or nice, but can also connote time spent with loved ones, seeing a friend after a long absence, or general togetherness." And you can feel that every time you walk into the shop.

Damascus Food Market

942 Hillside Avenue, Victoria | 250-595-8487
damascusmarket.ca | FB: Damascus Food Market

Salem Ajaj and his family came to Canada as Syrian refugees in 2016, but it was a circuitous route that had first led them to countries like Algeria, Lebanon, and Turkey before finding safe haven in Victoria. Even then, it took him three years to get to the point of being able to open the original location at the corner of Hillside Avenue and Cedar Hill Road. I recall that being a very cramped shop full of products but not much room to move around in. Now Damascus Food Market is firmly entrenched in a more spacious and modern building at Quadra and Hillside with even more products available to an ever-growing clientele, including meats and fresh fruits and vegetables. Everything is Halal. At the beginning, the people who frequented the store came from the small but growing Syrian community, but as more customers came along from Iran, Algeria, Morocco, Afghanistan, Pakistan, and Lebanon, he expanded his line of products to appeal to them. As we walked down the aisles of the shop, Salem explained how he now carries hundreds of different spices and spice blends, and dozens of different oils, dates, tea, honey, and more. And with a greater interest in Middle Eastern cooking spawned by chefs like Yotam Ottolenghi, more people like me show up to find ingredients. On one recent visit, I picked up a bottle of cherry molasses, which I had never heard of before, and a tray of delicate phyllo pastries stuffed with ground walnuts and sweet cheese and topped with ground pistachios. Salem explained the pastries are made by new immigrant families in Victoria as they always need to pick up some extra money when they first arrive.

Salem Ajaj.

Fig Mediterranean Deli

1551 Cedar Hill Cross Rd, Victoria | 250-727-3632

Yasser Youssef.

If someone asks me about Fig Deli, the first story I usually tell them is the time my wife and I went there and picked up a loaf of their olive bread, which was still warm out of the oven. We thought it would last us for a couple of meals. Wrong. I think it was gone within an hour of getting home. The baked goods are just one of the attractions of Fig, a well-stocked Mediterranean deli and lunch spot that you would very likely miss if you were driving down Cedar Hill Cross Road toward Shelburne and its collection of chain supermarkets. The store occupies one side of the strip mall which also contains a Salvation Army Thrift Shop, a Korean grocery store (also worth a visit), and Japanese restaurant. It's been in this location for about a dozen years now, a much larger place than the original store founded by Yasser Youssef, a Lebanese immigrant who fled the civil war in Lebanon to arrive in Canada in 1985. While he was working in restaurants in Victoria he found out there might be a need for a shop that could provide ingredients people were looking for, and Fig was born. The great thing about living in Victoria, though, is that if you provide a great place for ingredients from one area of the world, people might get you to bring in foodstuffs from different areas. As the immigrant population expanded in Victoria, Youssef now stocks some Ukrainian and Slavic items, and now at Christmas time you may find some European Christmas products like panettone from Italy and German stollen and lebkuchen. Fig is not big on social media but is big on word of mouth, which is just like social media but without the internet, right?

For Good Measure

3831 Cadboro Bay Road, Victoria | 250-477-6811
579 Niagara Street, Victoria | 250-385-1719
forgoodmeasure.ca

For Max Young, the world of bulk food and roasting nuts came to him early in life as he started working in his father's For Good Measure bulk food store founded in Cadboro Bay in 1985 when he was fifteen years old. In the early 2000s, they started roasting nuts and eventually opened the Island Nut Roastery in Sidney (6–2042 Mills Road, islandnutroastery.com). When he took over the business from his father in 2013, Max decided to grow the business by taking the nuts they were roasting and grinding them into butter so locals would have a source that they knew was small batch, fresh, and free of any additives. Now the Island Nut Roastery produces peanut, almond, and cashew butters as well as an almond hemp butter. All the nuts are hand-roasted in big ovens before being ground to butters or added into some of the signature snack mixes Island Nut Roastery has become known for that have such BC West Coast names like the Sunshine Coast, Sea to Sky, Strathcona, and One-Sailing Wait trail mixes. Meanwhile back at the original Cadboro Bay location of For Good Measure, you might still see Max's parents now and then as they deliver fresh produce to the store from their farm in Cobble Hill. In 2020, Max started operating the store at 579 Niagara Street in James Bay as a second For Good Measure location. This building has been in continuous use as a grocery store since about 1910, and Max has continued the tradition by continuing to offer fresh and local produce there are well as the bulk foods. It even has a sunny patio out back called the Hideaway, where you will find local musicians playing from time to time during good weather. While the store has changed hands and names many times over its 115 years of operation, it's good to see it continuing with a firm local tradition.

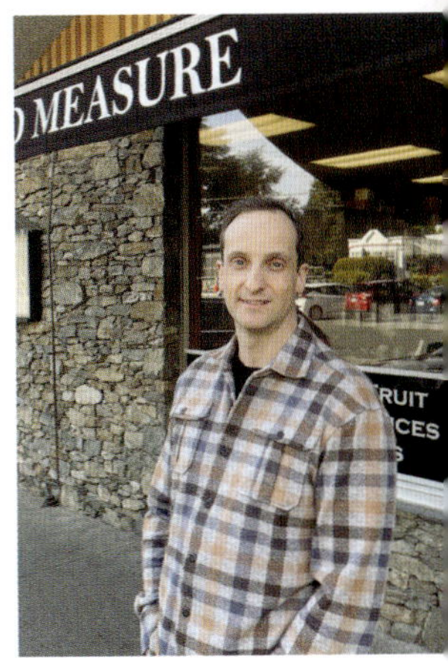

Max Young at For Good Measure Cadboro Bay.

The Local General Store

1440 Haultain Street, Victoria | 778-265-6225
thelocalgeneralstore.ca | IG: haultaingeneral

The year after the first edition of this book was published, I moved to Victoria from Cobble Hill. I soon discovered that just a block away from my new address was Haultain Corners, a neat little hub of independent businesses, including the Local General Store, and it stocked many of the products from artisans in the book! I met the then-owners, Alix and Chris Harvey, both retired educators. The store was supposed to be a gentle part-time occupation to ease into retired life, but they both admitted it easily became full-time jobs for them. Outside the store are bins and shelves of local produce in season. Breads arrive from neighbourhood bakeries, and there are dairy products from island producers. Inside the aisles are narrow and cramped, which will remind older readers of old-style general stores where you could find everything you needed if you just looked for it long enough. The shop opened in 2013, and by 2023 the Harveys were ready to let go of their first retirement project. Matt Humphrey and Meagan Crosby, one of the original employees at the store, took over as joint owners, and their mission remains the same as the Harveys' original vision of the shop: an old-fashioned general store where you can buy local products and be told the stories behind them.

Matt Humphrey.

The Market Garden

810 Catherine Street, Victoria | 250-384-7023 | rttownsend.com

The Market Garden is the creation of Ryan Townsend, who has a background in craftsman design and construction. His creative talent really shows, as when you walk into the Market Garden, it is unlike walking into any other grocery store you've ever been in. First, there's the piano. A big grand one, and not just for decoration, occasionally someone will tinkle the ivories there. Then there are the chandeliers and other light fixtures, definitely not standard issue. Huge mirrors, vaulted ceilings, and antique tables used as shelving fill up the space. The displays of local and imported goods are as artfully arranged as any fancy display I've seen in the UK or Europe. There is an enormous amount of care that goes into both the provisioning and merchandising of this shop, which is a bit of a warren of different rooms, each of which offers up sections of specialties, be it Italian nougat and panettone, or preserved food products created by local food artisans. They're trying to cut down on packaging, and many of the dry goods there are available in bulk to be refilled in your own containers. Don't forget to check the little downstairs rooms as well for additional delights. And there is a garden behind the store, originally run as a seed company.

Ryan Townsend.

The Market Stores

Market on Yates: 903 Yates Street, Victoria | 250-381-6000
Market on Millstream: 125-2401C Millstream Road, Victoria | 250-391-1110

Many years ago, when I was involved with the making of an artisan food product myself, it was time to start selling to retailers and the advice was "call Ernie Skinner. He'll probably carry it." And the advice was good. Ernie Skinner, co-founder of the Thrifty Foods chain and the founder of the Market Stores, was definitely a supporter of local artisans trying to get the word out on their goods. Ernie actually "retired" from Thrifty Foods in 1991, but by 1999 he was back in business with the Market on Yates, and in 2006 he opened the Market on Millstream with his daughter and son-in-law. These are supermarkets with a difference—special attention is paid to particular departments in the store, like fresh meats, seafood, and poultry, and there is an especially nice range of organic produce. Go for a wander, and you'll always find something you haven't seen anywhere else. It's not often you can find larger-sized grocery stores with such a variety in their product lines. Supermarket chains tend to go with the biggest name brands as well as their own "store" brands, but the Market Stores excel at bringing in grocery items you just don't see anywhere else, like the bison products in their meat department.

Mexican House of Spice

1412 A Douglas Street, Victoria | 250-388-6602
FB: Mexican House of Spice

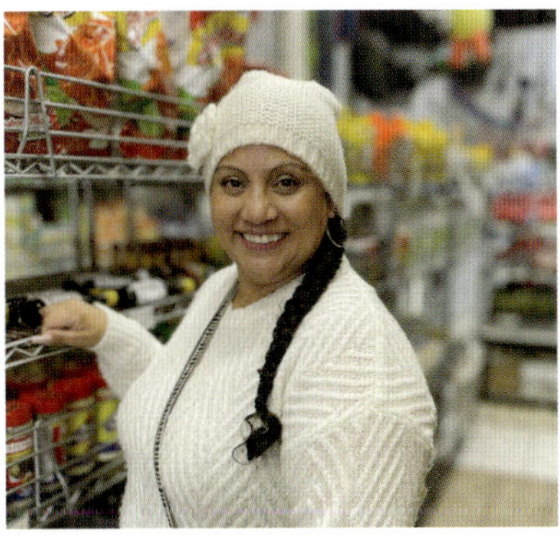

Maritza Sanchez.

It's the kind of shop you could just walk by and not notice, especially when the sign above the store used to be for some sort of hair salon supply shop. But once you do walk into the Mexican House of Spice on Douglas Street, you'll never forget it. Although the name says Mexican, you will find dried—and sometimes fresh—goods like cactus leaves (nopalitos) from all over Latin America, Africa, and Jamaica, as well as queso fresco. The array of spices and chili powders is huge, and while I wasn't expecting to find it there, once I asked if they had ground cardamom, and they did and at a very decent price. The cooler is stocked with all kinds of soft drinks from as far away as Argentina, and it would be hard not to find the particular dried chillies you're looking for. The baked goods like empanadas are commissioned from recent arrivals to the Latin American community in Victoria, which has been steadily growing over the years. When store owner Maritza Sanchez moved to Victoria nearly forty years ago, she figured there were probably just four Latin American families. Now, the families that visit the House of Spice are coming from all over Vancouver Island.

Nootka Rose Milling

4480 Happy Valley Road, Metchosin | 250-800-1207
nootkarose.ca | IG: nootkarosemilling

Erika Heyrman of Wild Fire Bakery and Byron Fry of Fry's Bakery of Victoria both had a similar problem. They were milling their own grains inside their bakeries. They had discovered it's not ideal to be milling the grain and trying to bake at the same time. A year after they started talking about their problem, a solution presented itself when a space came up in an old auto repair shop in Metchosin, and Nootka Rose Milling was born. They ran it together for five or six years until Byron wanted to just concentrate on his baking, so Erika now runs the place but both bakeries pay Nootka Rose for the milling. Part of the deal with getting the space stipulated there had to be some sort of retail shop there as well. It took them a couple of years to get it going, but now there is a nice little shop beside all the grain storage and milling equipment that gets regular deliveries of baked goods from Fry's and Wild Fire while the various flours go back the other way. There are also a lot of local products, pork, chicken, and lamb from farms just down the road, honey made from Jordan River and Metchosin flowers, and of course a selection of freshly milled grains, including some grown on Vancouver Island, but never farther than the borders of British Columbia. While earlier in her career as a baker, Erika placed a high value on using organic grain, which often had to be shipped from very long distances. Now she places more emphasis on local, and how keeping the foodways of growing grain close to where you mill it, bake it, and eat is better from all perspectives than importing grain from long distances. Everyone works together. If there are breads left over that aren't suitable for donation for people to eat, those breads go to the pigs at local farms. They eat the bread, and then someday the pork turns up for sale at Nootka Rose.

Shawna Knight, Miller at Nootka Rose.

Ottavio Italian Bakery & Delicatessen

2272 Oak Bay Avenue, Victoria | 250-592-4080
ottaviovictoria.com | IG: ottavio.victoria

Ottavio is one of those shops that makes life so easy and so difficult. It's easy because you can go there for local and imported cheeses, deli meats, in-house baked bread and pastries, gelato, a wide range of high-quality processed foods, coffee, breakfast, or lunch. It's difficult because the selection is so good, you have a hard time choosing what you want. I have a problem from the moment I step in the door. Do I go and check out the cheeses first? Or the olive oils and vinegars? The cookies? The house-made gelato? The grilled panini? This is a shop that requires repeated visits. The company was founded in 1997 by husband-and-wife team Andrew Moyer and Monica Pozzolo. They decided to sell Ottavio to a local hospitality group, but the new managers are long-time employees, and it remains one of my favourite places in Oak Bay. There's nothing like sitting on the multi-tiered patio in sunny weather, enjoying a cappuccino and a pastry. Even if it's a little chilly there are some overhead heaters to keep you warm.

YOU MIGHT ALSO WANT TO TRY:

The Italian Bakery, 3197 Quadra Street, Victoria (250-388-4557, italianbakeryvictoria.com). Its origins also stem from the Pozzolo family, and while not as expansive as Ottavio's, you will still find great breads, pastries, custom-made cakes, gelato, and coffee.

Italian Food Imports, 1114 Blanshard Street, Victoria (250-385-7923, italianfoodimports.ca). There is usually a line-up out the door here at lunchtime of people waiting for made-to-order deli sandwiches. Try the meatball sandwich. While you're waiting for your order, wander the aisles and scan the refrigerated counters for pastas and pestos, deli meats, and cheeses.

Pepper's Foods

3829 Cadboro Bay Road, Victoria | 250-477-6513
peppers-foods.com | IG: peppersfoodsvictoria

I have to admit I was very impressed the first time I walked into Pepper's Foods in Cadboro Bay. It doesn't present as a large store from the outside, but when you walk in, there are long aisles absolutely crammed. They stock not only grocery essentials but also a great variety of local and BC products, which starts in the fruit and vegetable section and extends into a fascinating array of many of the Island food artisans mentioned in this book—and even some I haven't heard of before! Take your time as you walk up and down the aisles, as there is lots to look at in every department, fresh, dried, canned, you name it. Their website says it all: "Pepper's Foods is 100 percent locally owned. We have a passion for food and are committed to offering locally and ethically sourced products." I started going there a few years ago when a friend started handling their social media and told me about the store, but I kept on going once my wife and I bought e-bikes, as Cadboro Bay became a favourite destination for the exercise, the beach and its views, and the ability to go into Pepper's and get everything I need for a picnic in the park. Students with appropriate ID can get a 10 percent discount every day, and seniors get the same treatment on Tuesdays and Wednesdays. Pepper's Foods has consistently received Awards of Merit and Best in BC awards in their category from the Canadian Federation of Independent Grocers over the almost quarter-century the store has been in operation.

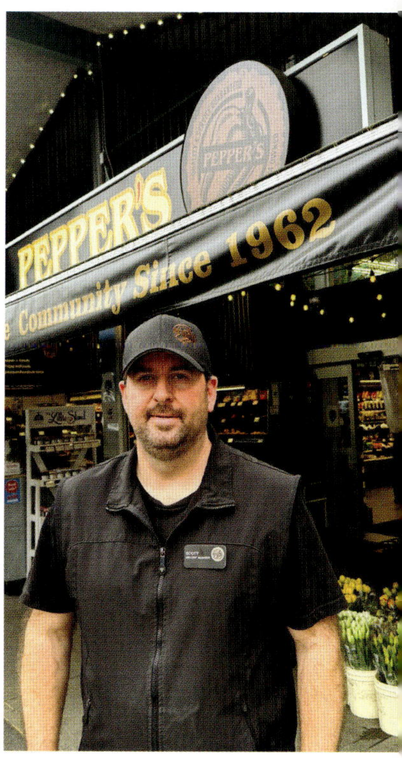

Scott Zaichkowsky, Pepper's Grocery Manager.

» Pepper's Foods

YOU MIGHT ALSO WANT TO TRY:

A number of small grocery store chains and individual shops have started up in the south Vancouver Island area over the past few years and managed to buck the big box trend that previously swept most of Canada. The stores are locally owned and managed by people who may have started out with the big ones but wanted to offer something individually crafted to the customers in their area. And they have been thriving. Here are a few that are definitely worth a visit!

- **The Old Farm Market**, Courtenay, Duncan, and Oak Bay (theoldfarmmarket.ca)
- **Red Barn Markets**, eight stores in the Greater Victoria and Saanich Peninsula region (redbarnmarket.ca)
- **Urban Grocer**, Victoria (urban-grocer.ca)

The Root Cellar Village Green Grocer

271 Cook Street, Victoria | 778-265-8166
1286 McKenzie Avenue, Saanich | 250-477-9495
therootcellar.ca | IG: rootcellar

I had often driven by the Root Cellar without dropping in until a friend told me it was the best place to find the large quantities of produce I needed for my various canning projects. They were right. From the first time I went in, I was hooked. Adam and Daisy Orser put together a huge variety of fresh produce in their original shop on McKenzie Avenue. There is an emphasis on local, especially during the growing season, then BC, and then beyond, when they need to provide products that people want, especially in the organic range. The original store underwent a huge expansion in 2013 when they took over a plant nursery next door and, among other improvements like a coffee shop, installed a full-service butcher shop (called the Chop Shop) stocked with local meats. "I brought in three real butchers to run the counter," Adam told me. "These are guys who have worked right from the abattoir level to the retail trade, so they know what they're doing." With demands for a shop closer to downtown Victoria, a smaller version of the Root Cellar opened in 2021 in Victoria's Cook St. Village, taking over the old Oxford Foods location at the corner of Oxford and Cook. It immediately fit very well into the neighbourhood and made it difficult for me to decide which location to go to! Definitely the original during canning season as they will often sell case lots of tomatoes, then Cook Street during the winter just because it's closer to my house, and I can easily ride my bike there and enjoy some of the other great shops in Cook St. Village. Root Cellar has also created their own house brand called Common, but they call the products under that label Uncommonly Good. You'll find both jarred and canned goods, peanut butter, coconut milk, big jars of spices, and more. I just cracked open a jar of their organic tomato and basil pasta sauce and tasted it while I put the pasta on to boil for a simple dinner, and the early reports are good!

Daisy and Adam Orser.

Victoria Olive Oil Company

619 & 617 Broughton Street, Victoria | 778-265-5045
victoriaoliveoilco.ca | IG: victoriaoliveoilco

Cherilee Dick.

■ **All around Vancouver Island,** and across Canada for that matter, you will find shops that share the same distributor of high-quality olive oils and vinegars, all available from bulk stainless-steel containers called fusti. The similarity stops there, though. Each shop has its own unique name and décor and chooses the other products which round out its offerings. In Victoria that shop is called the Victoria Olive Oil Company, and I think it's one of the best. As usual, you can taste every single oil or vinegar direct from its fusti to determine if it's to your liking. I am very partial to the blood orange olive oil, made from crushing the oranges and the olives together as opposed to a "flavouring" added to the oil. Among the vinegars the Sicilian Lemon White Balsamic is a fave, but on one of my visits Cherilee Dick got me to try a little taste of Cranberry-Pear White Balsamic mixed with a lemon-infused olive oil. Wonderful! Cherilee had been working in the Nanaimo location of Olive This & More when the opportunity arose to take over the Victoria location, and she and her husband Kevan jumped at the opportunity. Since then, they have expanded into the storefront next door at 617 Broughton and Cherilee's merchandising skills really started to shine as they now had twice the original space to work with. While there are high quality condiments and sauces and pastas and dry goods from all over the world to choose from, Cherilee has also carefully curated many products from local food artisans, so it's a go-to source to find something new to you and/or locally produced as well as fulfilling all your oil and vinegar needs.

Well Provisioned

Victoria | wellprovisioned.ca | IG: wellprovisioned.ca

Well Provisioned is a Victoria-based company that puts together people who want to give the perfect gift with local artisans who work hard creating their products. Amber Shute is both an entrepreneur and a long-time foodie with a background in the hospitality business. Like many other businesspeople during the pandemic of the early 2020s, she was looking to pivot to something new and decided to combine her acumen with sleuthing out local products with a service to help people short of time and imagination.

While Amber puts together packages with locally produced wellness products, it's her food packages that are of course the most attractive to me. She has pre-made pizza, grilling, and charcuterie essentials baskets but also can create custom food baskets packed with her favourite locally produced goodies. Businesses are fond of using Well Provisioned to gift clients at the end of projects, while Mother's Day proves to be popular with individuals looking for the perfect gift for Mom.

Amber Shute.

The Wooden Shoe

2576 Quadra Street, Victoria | 250-382-9042 | woodenshowdeli@shaw.ca
woodenshoedeli.ca | FB: Victoria Woodenshoe Deli

Somehow there always has to be something Dutch in my life. My best friend from high school is of Dutch heritage. So was my first wife. The documentary producer I worked with for many years on Vancouver Island is Dutch. So it's not surprising that I picked up a taste for many Dutch and Indonesian Dutch foods. These include somewhat odd things that many other Canadian do not profess a liking for. Luckily for me, there has been a Dutch specialty shop in Victoria since the 1950s, so I can get all those odd things, like salted licorice, rollmops (pickled herring rolls), fiery sambalulek (Indonesian chili paste), and sweets like stroopwafel (thin waffle and syrup biscuits), and around Christmas time, chocolate letters for the first initials of all of our family and friends. All this and much more can be found in a packed little shop on Quadra Street called The Wooden Shoe, family owned and operated since 1956. The founding Olivier family sold the shop in 2019 to then-employee Nicolette van Zoolingen and her husband Eric. There is always a friendly smile and hello when I walk in the door, and in the large alcove on the far side of the shop, seventy-five different kinds of licorice await. Cheese fanatics can choose from more than twenty kinds of Dutch cheese. My favourite is the Gouda spiced with cumin seeds.

Nicolette and Eric van Zoolingen.

SATURDAY SOJOURN

So many options, so little time. This is just one way I would spend my day in the city. Because I am of Italian heritage, I would start at **Ottavio** in Oak Bay—a cappuccino, a pastry, and the Pursuits section of *The Globe and Mail* get me going. Food columnist Julie Van Rosendaal or a guest chef may have a recipe that inspires me for a Sunday dinner, but ingredient gathering starts today. If the recipe has any Italian or European overtones, it's likely I can find what I need right there at Ottavio in the way of cheeses, pastas, and any special flavourings like capers or anchovy paste. From Ottavio, a quick wander down the street into the building that houses both the **Whole Beast Salumeria** and the **Village Butcher**. At the **Whole Beast**, Cory Pelan might tempt me with some truffled sausage or perhaps a Chinese-style pork belly, while the folks behind the counter at the Village Butcher will offer up a locally raised chicken or perhaps cut a piece of brisket just the way I like it for brining and smoking at home.

Head downtown and walk between my two favourite places to find cookbooks: **Russell Books** on Fort Street and **Munro's Books** on Government Street. Russell has a wide selection of used and out-of-print cookbooks and books on general gastronomy; Munro's is where I find all the latest and greatest in food, including some of my favourite food magazines. I usually leave with a heavy tote bag full of books.

If you have one more bag with you, and still have an arm to carry something, visit with Cherilee Dick on nearby Broughton Street and the **Victoria Olive Oil Company**. Cherilee or one of her staff will lead you through a tasting of the many types of high-quality olive oils and balsamic vinegars they have to offer, in the tasting room, and then go right next door for another pleasing array of imported and local foodstuffs, including hot sauces, spice rubs, pastas, and much, much more.

This is just one of the ways I would spend my Saturday in Victoria when food is the main focus.

Saanich Peninsula

Brentwood Bay
Saanich
Saanichton
Sidney

5

SAANICH PENINSULA

I had the good fortune of getting to know the Saanich Peninsula many years before I moved to Vancouver Island. My ex-wife's parents lived here, and when we would visit from Vancouver, we would often hop on spare bicycles they had stored in the garage. Since they lived in the Quadra/Mackenzie area, we would hook up with the Lochside Trail, get into the Saanich Peninsula, and cycle past the infamous Lochside pigs wallowing in the mud of the sty—search for Lochside pigs on Instagram, and you'll see they're still there! Where I started to appreciate how the peninsula was a special climate was when we cycled by kiwifruit orchards and stopped on the side of the trail or roads for a feast of blackberries. Michell's Farm with its vast pumpkin fields would be there in the fall, and Mattick's Farm was a stop for tea and goodies. Getting all the way out to Sidney meant a stop for lunch at the Blue Peter Pub (since burned down). To get home sometimes we'd cycle all the way back on West Saanich Road and stop at various farmers' markets . . . which is probably a very dicey proposition on bikes these days given the increase in traffic. Now it's usually hopping in the car to do a trip out to Dan's Farm and Country Market, Gobind Farms for berries, and perhaps Sea Cider for a tasting and snacks. While there has been a lot of light industrial and housing development taking place on the peninsula, there is still lots of green space to enjoy, including hikes around Elk and Beaver Lakes, and there's always the Centre of the Universe to enjoy at the Dominion Astrophysical Observatory.

Swartz Bay
North Saanich
McDonald Park Rd
Resthaven Rd
Four Quarters Meats
Mills Rd
Sidney
Beacon Ave
Muffet & Louisa
17
West Saanich Rd
Highway 17
Sea Cider Farm and Ciderhouse
Saanich Organics
Mt Newton Cross Rd
West Saanich Rd
Silver Rill Berry Farm
Saanichton
Hovey Rd
Wallace Rd
Saanichton Farm
Stelly's Cross Rd
Carnivore Meats & More
West Pacific Seafoods
Brentwood Bay
Central Saanich
Keating Cross Rd
Adriana's the Whole Enchilada
Level Ground Coffee Roasters
Triestina Pasta & Provisions
Sean Rd
Dan's Farm & Country Market
Berryman Farms AKA Berryman Brothers Meats
Bear Hill Rd
Dooley Rd
Wallace Rd
Oldfield Rd
Mosi Bakery
Gigi's Italian + Specialty Foods
Clairemont Ave
Cordova Bay Rd
17
West Saanich Rd
Royal Oak Rd
Blenkinsop Rd
Babe's Honey Farm & Fermentorium
Galey Farms
Saanich
Highway 17
Mckenzie Ave
2 km

FOOD ARTISANS OF THE SAANICH PENINSULA

Mosi Bakery Cafe & Gelateria

5303 West Saanich Road, Saanich | 250-590-7969
mosibakery.com | IG: mosibakery

Mosi Production Manager Chelsea Crossley.

It would be hard to do justice to the story behind the existence of the Mosi family operations in the limited space I have here. Suffice to say that Stefano and Melissa met in Victoria and got married over twenty-five years ago. Stefano arrived from Italy with his family, who had a bakery there during the Second World War. Melissa was a student in the Camosun College Culinary Program. Over the years they have owned and operated bakeries and gelato shops both on Vancouver Island and on Maui, Hawaii. Stefano's gelato skills are legendary. In 2019 he represented Mosi Gelato (their shop on Johnson St. in Victoria) in an American gelato competition and brought home the gold for his Seamist gelato, featuring Victoria's Silk Road peppermint tea as one of the ingredients. The gelato shop on Johnson closed down during the Covid-19 pandemic, but they kept going strong at the Mosi Bakery near Prospect Lake. That bakery opened in 2019 on their return from Hawaii in a hundred-year-old building that once was the local post office. They converted the top half of the house into the bakery, which also houses their gelato production. Down the street toward Victoria is Mosi Aquacotta, a dine-in café, featuring products from the bakery including some amazing sandwiches, and they grow fruits and vegetables and flowers for the café and bakery at the farm they bought just down the road a few years ago (which also has a farm stand). This is not a family that sits on its laurels. Another Mosi was scheduled to open in the spring of 2025 in Cordova Bay. They are most proud of their croissants, sourdough breads, and of course their gelato. Chelsea Crossley joined the Mosi team five years ago as their production and wholesale operations manager, and according to Melissa and Stefano, her pie knowledge is amazing, so don't forget to try the pies on your next visit.

Sea Cider Farm and Ciderhouse

2487 Mount St. Michael Road, Saanichton | 250-544-4824
seacider.ca | IG: seaciderhouse

There are more and more companies making authentic fruit ciders in British Columbia, but companies like Merridale and Sea Cider led the resurgence in crafting unique blends. This old beverage is steadily gaining new fans. I think our palates are becoming much more sophisticated now, and more people are looking for different taste experiences. Kristen Jordan at Sea Cider has persisted in marketing the image of cider as a sophisticated beverage, and it shows, not only in the taste of her products but also in the packaging, the decor of the ciderhouse, and the knowledge and professionalism of her staff. There are a couple of products of note. The Rumrunner cider is crafted from local heritage apples and then aged in rum barrels. If you visit, ask about Kristen's adventure in getting the barrels. And then there is the Kings and Spies cider, made mostly from King and Northern Spy apples gleaned from backyards in Victoria. In 2020 Sea Cider launched their non-alcoholic Temperance Series as Kirsten realized there was demand for craft non-alcoholic beverages. Sea Cider's Temperance Series consists of non-alcoholic sparkling juices which are free of added sugars. We quite often pick up a Temperance Chérie at a neighbourhood grocery store as a light way to start our meal. The farm is a great place to visit, especially in the fall when you can wander through the orchard in front of the cider house and see the cider apples ripening. Don't try to sample them, they are *not* apples you'd enjoy eating. After your wander, you can enjoy eating some small dishes inside the large tasting room to go along with glasses of cider designed to pair with the menu.

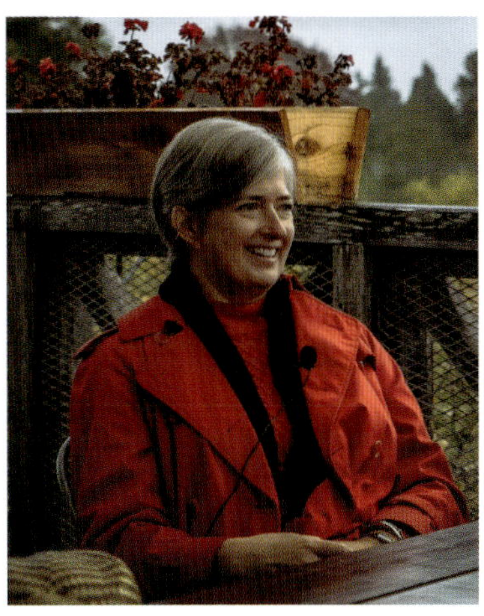

Kristen Jordan.

Berryman Farms a.k.a. Berryman Brothers Meats

2812 Dooley Road, Saanich | 778-351-3633

berrymanfarms.ca | FB: Berryman Brothers Meats LTD.

The Berryman family has deep roots on Vancouver Island, running back four generations now. The current generation of Berrymans consists of nine brothers, two sisters, and of course a huge extended family. Justin and Greg Berryman are at the helm of Berryman Brothers Meats and have an impressive butcher shop I've visited a few times to pick up steaks and chops as well as special orders I've made for good-sized pork bellies I use to brine and smoke my own bacon. Along with the custom cutting they do, the Berrymans make sausages and cured meats, meat pies, bone broth, even tourtières and marinated whole chickens . . . and more, including some seafood like scallops, prawns, and salmon. You can even buy whole suckling pigs if you're planning a backyard roast, and yes, they can rent you a fancy spit roaster too. Their website has an extensive shopping function, and I especially like the "Make a Meat Box" feature where you can select from one of their assortments or make up your own and have it delivered to your door, as far away as Qualicum Beach.

Greg and Justin Berryman.

Carnivore Meats & More

6–7103 West Saanich Road, Brentwood Bay | 778-351-4733
carnivoremeats.ca | FB: Carnivore Meats & More

Carnivore Meats Butcher Dave Corneau.

Carnivore Meats & More hit the ground running in Brentwood Bay back in 2014 with a dedication to carrying as much ethically raised, locally sourced meats as possible. That just wasn't that common in most butcher shops and grocery meat departments back then. The original founder of Carnivore, Ian MacDonald, emphasized that the beef and lamb available there were grass-fed and grass-finished, leading to better flavour and a healthier fat profile. Today, Ian's son Joey is carrying on that tradition with a butcher shop offering a selection of choices and the "More" part comes in with a shop full of products from around Vancouver Island, some of which are featured elsewhere in this book, like the Tofino Hot Sauce Co. and Island Farmhouse Poultry; they even carry specialty meat products made by other meat companies, like the Cherry Chorizo Salami from Haus Sausage Co. in Victoria. Carnivore makes a fine merguez sausage with spiced ground lamb from Parry Bay farm in Metchosin; and loukaniko, which marries some of my favourite flavours like garlic, fennel, and orange peel together with pork from Stillmeadow Farm, also in Metchosin. On every label of the fresh meat is the name of the farm where the animals were raised, how far away it is from Brentwood Bay (twenty-eight kilometres from Parry Bay Farm, twenty-nine kilometres from Stillmeadow Farm) and the fact that the lambs were grass-fed while the pigs were grain-fed, and both the sausage types I bought were gluten and dairy free with no nitrates added. That's an impressive amount of information to get when you buy a sausage, and the counter people at Carnivore are also happy to talk to you about where any of their products come from. Try getting that in your basic meat department of a big box grocery store.

Four Quarters Meats

205–2031 Malaview Avenue W, Sidney | 250-508-7654
fourquartersmeats.com | IG: fourquartersmeats

Geoff Pinch.

I only needed to look a little way back at Geoff Pinch's resumé to realize it made great sense for him to create his own space where he could put all he had learned about transforming meat into practise. He had been working with Cory Pelan at the Whole Beast in Victoria for a while, coming up with new sausages and terrines, and he had also worked at the legendary JN&Z Deli in Vancouver on Commercial Drive. When I lived in Vancouver, the aroma in that deli instantly took me into a magical world of smoked meats and sausages. If he learned his trade at those two places, well, that was good enough for me. Part of Geoff's goal of opening his own place was to do more wholesaling to other retail outlets and restaurants, so even if you can't make it to Sidney, chances are you can find Four Quarters Meats products in many independent grocery stores in the Greater Victoria and Gulf Islands region.

Level Ground Coffee Roasters

1757 Sean Heights, Saanich | 250-544-0932
levelground.com | IG: levelgroundcoffeeroasters

The four families who founded this company back in 1997 have increased it into a thirty-employee-strong workforce, now occupying their fourth production facility in Saanich—which houses their offices, roastery, and a very comfortable café. The roaster keeps emissions low, and because of all the different ways their waste can be reused, Level Ground has been "landfill-free" for over fifteen years. A large part of Level Ground's mandate is to help people learning about what can be a shifting definition of fair trade, which can depend on which certifying agency farmers belong to. Then there is direct trade, whereby the roasters buy beans directly from the farmers without a broker in the middle. Level Ground sources high quality beans from organic and fair-trade, small-scale farmers. In addition to the coffees, Level Ground also imports certified fair trade and organic tea, organic dried fruit, cane sugar, and cacao nibs. Once you start snacking on the dried mango, you'll never stop! Stacey Toews, one of the founders, told me they see themselves as a bridge between the producer community and the consumer community. Much of the company's packaging, especially the tea and dried fruits, features photos on every bag of the farmers consumers help support, and that's all part of telling their stories. Level Ground Trading now ships its products to stores and consumers across Canada.

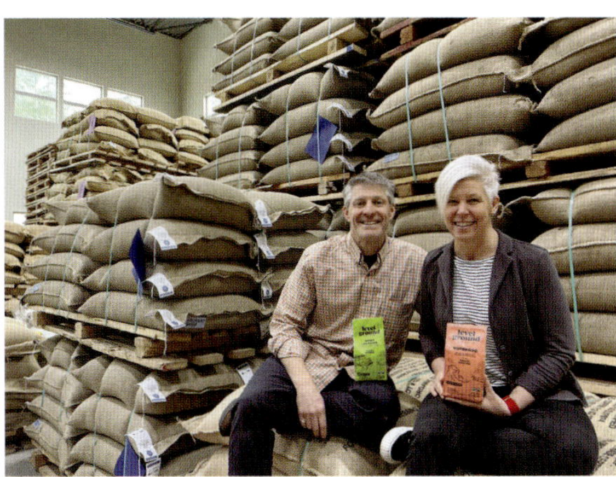

Level Ground Co-Founders Stacey Toews and Laurie Klassen.

muffet & louisa

Muffet & Louisa

102–2360 Beacon Avenue, Sidney | 250-656-0011 or 1-800-656-5575
muffetandlouisa.com | IG: muffetandlouisa

When Muffet Billyard-Leake opened her kitchenware store in Sidney nearly forty years ago, she named it after herself and her mother, Louisa. Now you know. But what you probably don't know is how she decided what to carry in the shop. Most people got their kitchen items from department stores or hardware stores, but Muffet thought that, while the range of items was vast, they weren't necessarily of such great quality. So instead, she satisfied her customers with less selection, but with top-notch quality. And while you can still shop for kitchen and dining items in Sidney at places like Canadian Tire and Home Hardware, Muffet & Louisa is still providing that "something different" in the shop on Beacon Avenue. And she has added other rooms of your house to her selections over the years. So along with the cookware and bakeware and kitchen tools you'll also find some gourmet food items, kitchen, bath, and bed linens, soaps, and body care. The Market Square version of the store closed years ago, but Muffet realized an easier place to expand was the internet. That's given her an even larger audience to draw from, but it's still nice to walk into a well-curated collection of things you need for your home.

o **Muffet Billyard-Leake.**

Nature Bee Wraps

Saanich | 250-415-6392
naturebeewraps.com | IG: naturebeegoods

Katie Gamble was travelling around doing internships at various companies during her studies at the University of Victoria's Gustavson School of Business when she discovered beeswax and cloth food wraps. Always thinking with sustainability in mind, she thought creating a business to manufacture and sell reusable food wraps would be a great final project. That was in 2018. She spent a lot of late-night sessions building the business in her parents' basement. She hadn't realized there were already other wrap businesses in the Greater Victoria, area but she was determined to carry on. Now Katie leads a team with three other women in a facility in Saanich that keeps her very busy.

The beeswax for the wraps comes from nearby Country Bee Honey Farm (countrybeehoney.ca) and is a reliable, local source. While she would love to source her fabrics for the wraps locally, it's one part of the product that needs to be imported from various countries as needed. The Covid-19 pandemic helped propel her business as people discovered her online store when they were looking for products to help preserve food and reduce waste with the enforced resurgence in home cooking.

From the food wraps Katie wanted to branch out into more products that could make life easier in the kitchen, bathroom, and laundry, using non-toxic and sustainably made ingredients. I think my favourites are the multi-purpose and bathroom cleaning tablets. You fill your spray bottle with warm water, drop in the tablet, let it fully dissolve, put the lid on and start spray cleaning. It works out to about half the price of a new bottle of cleaner and you can use your spray bottle over and over again. Nature Bee also offers foaming hand soap tablets, dishwasher tablets and reusable Swedish sponge cloths made from plant cellulose and recycled cotton. One of the newest products is a powder-to-gel dish soap, so you can cut down on your plastic bottles of that stuff, too.

I'm impressed with Katie's business acumen and how she has fully embraced all the different ways of promoting her product via social media. She told me her business school background has been a key to her success and her team and community are very important to her. She's not one to rest on her laurels but describes the necessity of adjusting to an ever-changing business climate as one of the most challenging parts of her career. Of course she's not afraid to get her hands dirty, because she knows how to clean up (pardon the pun!).

Left to right: Emily Mackin, Nature Bee Founder Katie Gamble, Sarah Gurney, Kami Manak.

Dan's Farm & Country Market

2030 Bear Hill Road, Saanichton | 250-652-9100
dansfarm.ca | FB: Dan's Farm and Country Market

Simon Fowler and son.

Dan's Farm & Country Market has been a fixture of my forays into the Saanich Peninsula ever since I discovered it was a great place to go to for authentic farm fresh food at decent prices. In fact, it has been in operation for over twenty-five years. It was a huge relief that both the farm and the store survived the Covid-19 pandemic because it could have easily gone the other way. Dan Ponchet himself was stranded in Peru when the big shutdown came . . . and the foreign workers that he depends on weren't able to get into Canada either, just as a crucial time of the farming season was arriving. But Dan's son-in-law Simon Fowler and the rest of the family and some of their friends pulled together to get through the worst of it, and today Dan's Farm & Country Market still offers the same things I've always gone there for—fresh baking, a freezer full of meats and sausages from area farms, and those very fresh veggies that may have been picked just a few hours previously. I have to remember to bring a lot of shopping bags with me because I always see something I hadn't planned on getting but then there it was for the buying, like big stalks of juicy rhubarb in the spring, then ripe tomatoes as the summer wears on, and maybe a big bag or even a box full of pickling cukes to make my own dill pickles. The farm operates over forty acres of land, and that gives them enough room for orchards to grow a dozen different varieties of apples and an equal number of different varieties of pear, including four types of Asian pears. Then there are six kinds of berries and umpteen different vegetables. It's the kind of farm we had in miniature at my house back in southern Ontario, a real mixed bag of fruits and vegetables that my mom and dad grew on an acre of land. Monoculture may have made sense from a strictly business point of view for huge farms, but farms like Dan's that mix it up will make it better for farmers and for their customers in the years to come.

Galey Farms

4150 Blenkinsop Road, Saanich | 250-477-5713
galeyfarms.net | FB: Galey Farms Corn Maze, Market and Railway

Galey Farms has become one of those great seasonal Victoria/Saanich institutions. You will find me there often during the height of the strawberry and raspberry seasons, which used to be berry brief (pardon the pun). I'm always checking their social media to see what they have to offer as the berries start coming in. Over the years, Galey has been planting more varieties of berries that are either everbearing or fruit longer into the summer and even into the fall. They have the Albion variety of strawberries that can be harvested close to the end of October—weather permitting—and they are especially sweet at that time of year. Other than the strawberries, raspberries, and blueberries, the veggie section comes on strong as well with zucchini and hard-skinned squashes, beets, carrots, onions and . . . well, just about all the standard vegetables you can ask for including corn—and yes, there is a corn maze, pumpkin field, and mile-long miniature train rides around the farm. Housed right beside the Galey Farms farmstand is Babe's Honey, so you can really stock up on lots of good things not far up the road from the Root Cellar at the intersection of Mackenzie and Blenkinsop. Be careful turning in and out of the Galey Farms parking lot, the traffic gets a little busy there in the summer!

Left to right; Ray, Rob, and Stephen Galey.

Saanich Organics

1438 Mount Newton Cross Road, Saanichton | 250-818-5807
saanichorganics.com | IG: saanichorganics

Left to right: Rachel Fisher, Heather Stretch, and Robin Tunnicliffe.

Saanich Organics is the product of three women who run farms in Saanich, along with some input from other organic or transitional organic farms in the Greater Victoria area. Robin Tunnicliffe of Feisty Field Organic Farm, Rachel Fisher of Three Oaks Farm, and Heather Stretch of Northbrook Farm are the heart and soul of Saanich Organics. They sell their products to residents through a weekly box delivery program, farmers' markets, and farm stands—as well as to restaurants and retailers. They earn their income from over a hundred different crops, so if a few fail because of pests or weather, there are always some backups in place. Their success comes from a combination of factors, including teamwork, hard work, and developing a sense of community. But it also has to do with growing their business in a part of the world where people are becoming much more concerned about where their food comes from and how it is produced. Heather says that even given that awareness, not everyone has caught on to the idea that this is the way we should be eating. "We still import the majority of the food we eat here on Vancouver Island," she says. "We need more farmers like us, and we need more people to think about eating more than just the fancy heirloom tomato that gets sliced on top of their industrially produced, imported greens." They are all about helping people grow their own food, and a few years ago, they started their own seed company called Seeds of the Revolution. I highly recommend the book they wrote together, *All the Dirt: Reflections on Organic Farming*, whether you are a new farmer, a backyard gardener, or just interested in how it's done. The book is packed with everything you need to know about organic farming.

Saanichton Farm

1947 Stelly's Cross Road, Saanichton | 250-727-1966 | saanichtonfarm.com

Bryce Rashleigh.

Bryce Rashleigh is a third-generation farmer; his grandfather came to Canada in 1912 and settled in Coombs, then Qualicum Beach, and finally to Saanichton in 1957. The farm was originally mixed-use and big on dairy, but like many of the other dairy farms on south Vancouver Island, they stopped growing grain and stopped milking cows and Saanichton was primarily a farm that grew hay for horses. It wasn't until the next generation of Rashleighs came along that the idea of growing grains again surfaced when Bryce's son went to agricultural college. "He's got the knowledge on how to run and fix the machines. We hooked up with some families in Alberta who have been a great help, almost like a sister-city kind of thing, every fall I go back to this little town, and I've learned more and done more." They would often have older, smaller equipment that they weren't using on their larger farms, so Bryce would bring it back and he and his son would fix it up and get it running again. Now they even have two stone mills to grind their wheat into flour they sell at the farm and various retailers. So, from a hay farm, they have moved into growing hard red spring wheat for bakeries and breweries and barley for breweries as well. Throw in turkeys, chickens, and eggs, and you have a mixed-use farm once again. Climate change is a concern. Frequent drought means crop yields are less, but Saanichton is doing what they can to "mitigate and adjust" their growing methods according to Bryce. The family is passionate about growing grains for the local market instead of importing food from far away. Their philosophy at Saanichton Farm? Growing and buying local food creates local jobs, supports the local economy, and reduces our environmental impact.

Silver Rill Berry Farm

1490 Hovey Road, Saanichton | 250-652-5227
silverrillberry.com | IG: silverrillberry

Pamela Fox.

When I was growing up, my parents grew their own raspberries and strawberries. They were the only berries I knew, and it wasn't until I moved to Vancouver Island much later in life that I learned a lot about blueberries and blackberries and finally, gooseberries and currants. As I found out from Pamela Fox, owner of Silver Rill Berry Farm in Saanich, currants are still to a certain extent very much a United Kingdom or European fruit, and through all the years she has grown them on her farm, she's had to explain what they are and their superior health benefits. "While these berries are well known to our European customers—black currants were given to kids during the wars because they're so high in vitamins—they aren't well known in North America because they were once banned in the US as the plant is a host to a disease that impacted the soft wood industry." The reason Pamela started growing them in the first place was kind of at the urging of her father. She had bought, from her father, part of the original farm in the Mount Newton valley that her family had farmed since 1915, and since it was on a dead-end road he said in order to attract customers to her crops she should grow something different. So she thought back to their English roots and planted red, black, and white currants, and some strawberries, gooseberries, jostaberries, and cherry trees as well—because who doesn't like cherries? A friend of mine up-island once asked me to come and help her pick a bumper crop of red currants. The hardest part was picking them off the stems. Pamela has two ways of dealing with that. Pick the berries and the stems, freeze them, and then the currants come off easily, and with no damage to their flavour or quality. They also have a very cool harvesting machine that slowly makes its way down the rows of bushes knocking berries off the bush and collecting them on a conveyor belt for inspection. Pamela has developed some value-added products as well, of course, including jelly, but she's very proud of a black currant concentrate she bottles that is very tasty and loaded with vitamin C, much more than in blueberries. In the past there have been collaborations with local breweries to create a black currant saison beer and a black currant blonde ale. Call the farm for selling locations and to order berries in advance.

Adriana's the Whole Enchilada

2140B Keating Cross Road, Saanichton | 250-652-7767
adrianasthewholeenchilada.com | IG: adrianasthewholeenchilada

Adriana Ramirez.

For the better part of three decades Adriana Ramirez has brought a taste of Mexico to as wide a swath of south Vancouver Island as possible. First at a small restaurant in Victoria and, for over twenty years now, at a storefront on Keating Cross Road that she opened with partner Wayne Adams. That location has a steady stream of customers coming in and then going out with armfuls of house-made corn and chia chips, tortillas, salsas, and pre-made meals you just pop into the oven and heat up. There are many different variations on tacos, taquitos, enchiladas, and quesadillas, empanadas, burritos, and soups. The other two sides of the business involve catering and a wholesale operation that distributes many of the dried and some of the fresh products to a couple dozen grocery stores up and down the Saanich Peninsula. Adriana's tries to source as many local products as possible to put into her dishes, and works closely with Dan's Farm, Michell's Farm, and Sun Trio Farms. To get a pinch of Mexico in your cooking, you just have to try Adriana's Magic Powder, a carefully mixed blend of paprika, chili powder, cayenne pepper, lemon pepper, oregano, some other secret spices, and salt.

Babe's Honey Farm & Fermentorium

4150 Blenkinsop Road, Saanich | 250-658-8319
babes-honey-farm.com | IG: babeshoneyfarm

Babe's Honey has been a household name for honey on Vancouver Island for nearly eighty years. It is known for being a high-quality local product as well as for its bright fluorescent-coloured labels. Charlie Warren and his wife, Alison, also known as Babe, ran the company for decades, starting in 1945 with just a few hives. Eventually they had thousands of hives positioned around Vancouver Island to allow bees to produce honey from all the wonderful flowers we have around here. After Charlie and then Babe passed away, the company eventually went into receivership, and the honey supply dried up. But Babe's Honey came back. Brandon Schwartz used to work at Babe's, and he didn't want to see all the bees, hives, and other equipment go to waste. He stepped in, with some financial help from his father, and bought the name and everything else he could afford at auction. Brandon set up shop at the Galey's Farm stand on Blenkinsop Road and rebuilt the business, and people were glad to see those bright labels coming back. What's been added to the line of products over the past few years are sparkling cultured honey drinks called Babe's Sparkling Beeline. Flavours include Currantly Hip, Mermaid Tears, Ginger, and Earl Grey. Brisk and refreshing! At the Galey's Farm shop, you can taste all the honeys and drinks before you buy, and the shop smells great, not only from the honey, but from all the beeswax candles available as well.

Triestina Pasta & Provisions

107–1753 Sean Heights, Saanichton | lapastatriestina.com
IG: lapastatriestina

Massimo Buggini.

When Massimo Buggini first met Susie Matthews, she didn't speak Italian, and he didn't speak English. But since they met in Spain, they found Spanish in common, and for a dozen years now they have been making beautiful food together. Massimo had been a chef in Italy and worked around the world. Susie is British, but her parents were living in Victoria when she and Massimo decided to join them here. Massimo has been perfecting his craft for years and is fiercely proud of using local ingredients like freshly milled organic wheat to make his pasta by hand. The pastas change with the season, summer will find local basil in his tagliatelle and the hand-milled passata (tomato puree) is made using Sun Wing farm San Marzano and Roma tomatoes. The provisions angle is intriguing as well. Massimo has developed a line of Italian-style baked goods like biscotti and soft amaretti that I find indistinguishable from the treats I enjoyed while living in Italy. You will find them often at the farmers market in James Bay, but in their small shop in Saanichton they have also brought in a line of superior Italian and Spanish food products like vinegars, olive oils, and canned fish.

Ultimate Microgreens

Saanich | 250-812-8082
ultimatemicrogreens.ca | IG: ultimatemicrogreens

Luis Sanchez and Dallas Elia started Ultimate Microgreens in 2019 having been disappointed in their winter garden attempts to provide them with fresh greens year-round. They had been experimenting with growing microgreens since 2013. Then Luis met a man through Facebook Marketplace who was leaving Canada and wanted to sell his equipment used for sprouting seeds and all his seed inventory. It was a good price, but Luis and Dallas ended up with six hundred kilograms of organic seeds! It was so much they could hardly make a dent in using that many. They were still in their original packaging, so they donated them to a food bank that put them to good use. The tiny sprouts they grow now are not grown in soil but a growing medium that allows them to be easily harvested after seven to eighteen days depending on the variety. When you buy their popular salad blend, you will get a variety of sprouts ranging from a variety of peas and radishes, broccoli and kohlrabi too. Right now, they are growing the sprouts in two different attached compartments; one is an old garage that Luis stripped right down to the studs and replaced the drywall with plywood painted with a special mould-resistant paint. A tunnel connects the garage to a shipping container. The light, heat, airflow, and humidity are all carefully controlled to produce a high-quality product. The majority of locally owned grocery stores in the Greater Victoria area are now carrying their microgreens, bringing them closer to their ultimate goal of providing all of Vancouver Island with fresh, healthy, and naturally grown microgreens.

Dallas Elia and Luis Sanchez.

Vumami Foods

Sidney | 250-689-5539 | vumamifoods.com | IG: vumamifoods

I just grabbed a jar of Nick Baingo and Lauren Isherwood's Umami Bomb Shiitake Chili Oil out of my fridge. It's almost empty, meaning it's time to stock up again. I don't know why I picked up a jar of this for the first time at a specialty grocery store, but I'm glad I did. I think it might have been the promise on the label: "Bring Bold, Savoury, Spicy Flavour to Any Dish." And it does. Boy, does it ever. It's hot, but it doesn't blow the top of your head off, and it definitely has a lot of umami. Umami translates from the Japanese as "pleasant, savoury taste" and entered into the foodie lexicon in the mid-2000s, joining sweet, salty, sour, and bitter as a *fifth* taste. It's kind of hard to describe, but it can be found in things as diverse as shiitake mushrooms, soy sauce, monosodium glutamate, tomatoes, and potatoes. When Nick and Lauren were travelling in South Korea, they ate at a vegan Buddhist restaurant and were amazed at the selection and flavours. Like me, they are lifelong condiment hoarders and they wanted to create something they could add to their vegan meals to recreate the delicious food they had in Korea. Through much trial and error, they finally came up with a palate-pleasing blend of spices, fermented bean paste, and shiitake mushrooms. It doesn't look like much in the jar, a thick, dark paste, but it really works to liven up almost any meal you can think of. They are now up to six different products, including Extra Hot, Hot, Medium in the original Umami Bomb, and then Sweet Heat, Garlic, and their newest, Tingly Szechuan. All products are keto and vegan and found in hundreds of shops across Canada.

Nick Baingo and Lauren Isherwood.

West Pacific Seafoods

7103 West Saanich Road, Brentwood Bay | 250-896-6685
700 Industrial Way, Tofino | 250-725-2244
westpacificseafoods.com | IG: westpacificseafoods

Brent Whitaker.

West Pacific Seafoods began life in Tofino in 2002 when Lutz Zilliken created a place where local fishermen could bring their catch which in turn provided locals with an opportunity to purchase from a reliable source of high-quality seafood. Over the years that business expanded to supplying restaurants with processed fish and a place that fishing lodges could send their customers to get their catches smoked, candied, or frozen. Brent Whitaker, now the director of operations at West Pacific Seafoods, got to know Lutz when Brent was the sous chef at Tofino's Wickaninnish Inn. As a fine dining chef by trade, Brent got talking to Lutz about all facets of the seafood industry. When Covid-19 hit, he started spending more time with Lutz as the restaurant was shut down. He learned to respect Lutz's insistence on fish that is ethically sourced and of the best quality. That's when Brent decided to leave restaurant kitchens behind and bought into West Pacific Seafoods as Lutz's partner. After much consideration and planning, Brent brought West Pacific's second location into existence in Brentwood Bay in July of 2023. He has a good neighbour, located right beside Carnivore Meats & More in a strip mall that seems to have all the basic necessities of life. Brent knew he picked the right location because as he was labouring away at the renovations, at least a dozen people would poke their heads in the door every day to ask what was under development there, and they all promised to show up when he opened. It's rare these days to have a stand-alone seafood shop in a smaller town, but people seem to be liking it, and with Brent's background as a fine dining chef, he's added a lunch component to the shop so you can go in and grab a decidedly better than average smoked salmon bagel sandwich.

Gigi's Italian & Specialty Foods

105–5118 Cordova Bay Road, Saanich | 236-475-8792
gigisitalianfoods.com | IG: gigisitalianfoods

Over a century ago, if you lived in Victoria and you wanted to visit the seaside resort of Cordova Bay, it meant a journey by train and stagecoach. It is decidedly easier to get back and forth these days, and Cordova Bay is very much a thriving community that is growing by leaps and bounds . . . which provided a business opportunity for Genna Purcell and her family. "We are Italian and growing up we would always have to venture to Vancouver for all our favourite products. We always felt that there was no one-stop shop locally for all our Italian needs. During the pandemic, we were unable to go to Vancouver and really missed certain ingredients and Italian products . . . so here we are today!"

Genna Purcell.

A few years in now, they continue to bring in new products from Italy and Europe every few weeks. The shop is generously sized and well-merchandised, so it doesn't feel crowded, but Genna says often return customers will come in and remark that they came when Gigi's first opened and they can't believe how many new products they have to offer. "Most of our products are made in Italy or Europe, probably ninety percent of our inventory. The quality is the closest thing you'll find outside of Italy. Our burrata gets flown in from Puglia almost weekly, and our Pecorino Romano is made from the last manufacturer standing in the Rome area." The only problem they have with a business that imports a lot of foods is the supply chain letting them down sometimes. That being said, there is lots of fresh food created there for customers like sandwiches and baked treats, even some custom-baked Italian-style doughnuts from Victoria's Doughnut Vault.

SATURDAY SOJOURN

This is another region of Vancouver Island that you can't really do justice to in one day, so you might want to plan an overnight stay. Or if you're based in Victoria, make sure you get out there on a regular basis on the weekends, especially at the height of the harvest season. Skip breakfast at home and make an early beeline for **Mosi Bakery**. Grab coffee and a pastry to enjoy inside but if the sun is out they have a nice little patio out front. Before you leave pick up a loaf of bread or a nice slab of focaccia. Nearby Mosi you will find **Dan's Farm Market** with a great selection of produce grown on that farm or others on the Saanich Peninsula.

For even more ingredients for a dinner, the **North Saanich Farm Market** or **Peninsula Country Market** should be your next stop. If a market is closed for the season, you can still check the website for vendors who have farm-gate shops or pop-up market sales in the off-season.

As you make your way back down the peninsula, check out **Muffet & Louisa** on Beacon Avenue in Sidney for the latest in kitchenware and linens. For a late lunch and tasting session, the **Sea Cider** ciderhouse is tucked behind an apple orchard not far from the Mount Newton Cross Road turnoff from the Pat Bay Highway. Taste the full range of ciders in short or long flights as you nibble on their Artisan Lunch Plate, which features BC-made meats and cheeses. When you're full of food, walk it off amidst the splendid foliage of the **Butchart Gardens**, where you can get enough exercise to work up your appetite once again for afternoon tea. Reservations recommended.

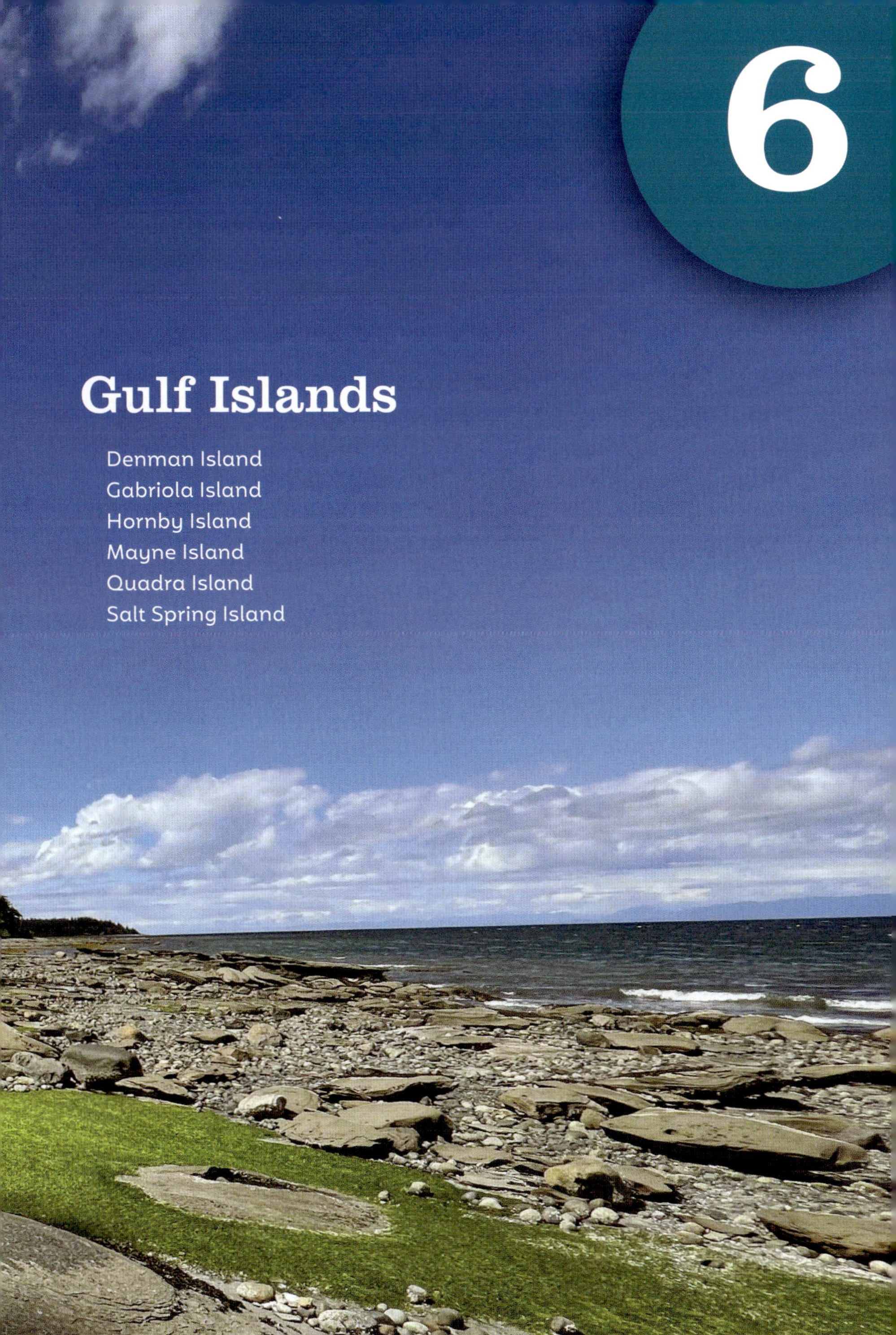

6

Gulf Islands

Denman Island
Gabriola Island
Hornby Island
Mayne Island
Quadra Island
Salt Spring Island

GULF ISLANDS

I haven't been to every habitable Gulf Island in BC, but I've got a nice sampling under my belt. They are truly magical places—you just get a different feeling when you arrive. Some people might describe it as being on island time, but for me I think it's just the knowledge that you're entering into a place that is, by its very nature, somewhat isolated from the rest of the world and sometimes that is a very good place to be. The islands never fail to surprise me with the kinds of entrepreneurial spirits who turn up there. Denman Island has a high-quality chocolate bar maker known across Canada. Then there's my friend Shirley Phillips of Lilac Sun Pottery who will sometimes set a fire in her driveway to glaze her pottery using a mixture of ingredients like coffee grounds, banana peels, seaweed, dried manure, and orange peels to get the desired result of a wild melange of colours setting into the clay. Tucked away in a forest on Hornby Island is a still distilling some of the finest gin I've ever tasted. Meanwhile on Saturna, Salt Spring, and Pender Islands, olives are being grown, and some of them have even been pressed to create a few precious litres of oil. I miss visiting the late Ken Stefanson, the Gabriola Gourmet Garlic guy, because he was a constant source of great chit chat and advice whenever I met him. "Plant your garlic in mid-October, under the light of the full moon, buck naked!" He told me that was sure to guarantee a healthy harvest. I guess I've been to Salt Spring Island the most. The Saturday market there is a favourite place to visit, and I've met many amazing artisans there who make everything from cheese, to bread, to jams, to tofu, to knives . . . the list goes on and on. And the apples. Salt Spring Island used to be the apple capital of Canada. Near the beginning of the twentieth century, over 360 tonnes a year of apples were being shipped off the island. There are still hundreds of different varieties of apples being grown there. Check out the yearly apple festival in late September or early October. In other words, get thee to a Gulf Island!

Campbell River
Denman Rd
Denman Island Chocolate
Buckley Bay
Denman Island
Shingle Spit Rd
Central Rd
Roburn Rd
Island Spirits Distillery
Hornby Island
4 km
Comox
19
Buckley Bay
Inland Island Hwy
Parksville
Woodfire Spice
North Rd
Gabriola Island
Nanaimo
2 km
Outlandish Shellfish Guild
Quadra Island Fisheries
West Rd
Quathiaski Cove
Quadra Island
Island Highway
Campbell River
1 km
Nanaimo
20 km
Trans-Canada Hwy
Ladysmith
1
Salt Spring Island
Duncan
Vesuvius
Galiano Island
Ganges
Long Harbour
Pacific Prowler
Mouat's Housewares Store
Toynbee Rd
Salt Spring Seeds
Fulford-Ganges Rd
Beddis Rd
Village Bay Rd
Fernhill Rd
Village Bay
Farm Gate
Mayne Island
Prevost Island
Soya Nova Tofu Company
Moonshine Mama's Elixirs and Tonics
Upper Ganges Rd
Robinson Rd
South End Sausage
Francis Bread
The Woodshed
Salt Spring Sea Salt Ltd.
SaltSpring Kitchen Company
Salt Spring Gelato
Monsoon Coast Trading Company
50 m
Stewart Rd
Reynolds Rd
Salt Spring Island
Point Rd
Beaver
Salt Spring Island Cheese
Fulford Harbour
King Rd
The Woodshed
Salt Spring Mercantile
Otter Bay
Pender Island
4 km

FOOD ARTISANS OF THE GULF ISLANDS

Francis Bread

6–319 Upper Ganges Road, Salt Spring Island | 250-537-7296
francisbread.com | IG: francis_bread

Peter Hunt and Meghan Carr.

■ **Peter Hunt of Francis Bread** grew up on Salt Spring Island, but he was living in Vancouver and working in the hospitality trade when he met Meghan Carr, also working in hospitality. When he brought her home to meet his parents she was so taken with the island she wanted to move there. Meghan says, "Peter became bread obsessed a few years before we opened the bakery and worked for other people in bakeries to gain some experience. There was already some amazing bakers on the island, but we saw they were selling out in just a few hours at the market so we knew Salt Springers were hungry for more." So they started Francis Bread, a bakery that uses only organic grains grown in BC and milled just across the water at True Grain Bakery in Cowichan Bay. The oven is wood-fired and their faithful fans rave about their products. Along with a large variety of sourdough breads, they also make pastries. I could probably live outside the bakery doors just on this list of their offerings: croissants, pain au chocolat, almond croissants, ham and cheese croissants, and seasonal fruit Danishes. Don't forget the pastry swirl featuring sultanas plumped in Earl Grey tea and the cardamom brioche knots. If you want to make your own pizza they offer you the dough to make your life easier, and they can also make you lunch, featuring produce from local farms, and pasture-raised meats from Salt Spring or Vancouver Island. You can't get much more "100-mile diet" than that. And who is Francis? Meghan: "Francis is a family name, I guess on Peter's side but we wanted it to be sort of a character or a third party in the business. Francis is its own thing that is not directly either of us. Neither of us felt right having our own name in the title, and we don't need another bread pun out there in the world of bakeries, so we thought this was nice. We both get called Francis all the time though and just kind of roll with it."

Island Spirits Distillery

4605 Roburn Road, Hornby Island | 250-335-0630 | islandspirits.ca

It's difficult to distill the spirit you get when you hit the entranceway of this distillery on Hornby Island. After driving through the dense bush lining the gravel road, you come to a clearing and the cedar-shake-clad home of the Phrog line of spirits. The modest footprint of the distillery is a pleasant reminder of when spirits were distilled by small companies around the country instead of in today's massive factories, where speed and quantity rather than patience and quality rule. Peter Kimmerly, John Grayson, and Dr. Naz Abdurahman teamed up in the early 2000s to share their love of experimenting with distilling spirits, and their products win rave reviews from consumers and at tasting competitions. Their Phrog Gin and Phrog Vodka are named to celebrate the multitudes of singing frogs on the Hornby property—the spelling reflects the scientific nature of the trio, pH being the measure used to describe the level of acidity in a substance. I have sat at the comfortable tasting counter, admired the complex curves of the still, marvelled at the number of aromatic botanicals added to the Phrog Gin, such as juniper, coriander, cinnamon, and eleven more, and then sipped and relaxed. The vodka is very smooth. The gin changes with every sip, more of the aromatics being released as you swirl it in your mouth and expose it to air.

Peter Kimmerly.

Moonshine Mama's Elixirs and Tonics

130–344 Upper Ganges Road, Salt Spring Island | 778-353-3352
moonshinemamas.ca | IG: moonshinemamaselixirs

The name of the company sounds like something being hawked at an old-fashioned medicine show, but there's nothing old-fashioned about the products developed by Melinda Divers . . . even if she calls herself the Moonshine Mamanatrix on her business card. Melinda started developing tonics with turmeric as the main ingredient when she was diagnosed with Stage 3 cancer in 2011. She researched natural ways to reduce inflammation and boost her auto-immune system, hitting on turmeric—or more precisely, the curcumin pigment *inside* the turmeric—as the key ingredient. Melinda started working in her home kitchen to find the right combination to get curcumin into her system every day and hit upon juicing fresh, organic turmeric to make a concentrated elixir that could be added to other drinks, with ingredients like black pepper, lemon, and coconut oil that activate the beneficial properties of the curcumin. Not only did it work wonders for Melinda, this elixir was something people wanted to buy. From her kitchen, the company moved into a shipping container for a new home, and in 2024 moved into a 12,500 square-foot factory on Salt Spring to meet the demand for product. The original elixir is now available in other flavours like lemon, lime, and cranberry. There are shrubs or drinking vinegars and "Baby Mama Elixirs" designed to let you shoot it, sip it, or mix it with two doses in every little 60 mL bottle. New in 2024 are Canned Mamas that are ready to drink without any other

Melinda Divers.

mixing required. Growing a small company into a larger company with national distribution is no easy feat when you're doing it from Salt Spring Island. Turmeric sourcing has had to move from Jamaica and Hawaii to Peru and she orders pallets instead of cases, the same goes for jars. But Melinda wasn't content to stay small. "These elixirs have impacted my health in such a positive way I want as many people as possible to have access to it." The health claims are not snake oil either. You can follow links on her website to studies published on the US National Library of Medicine website. I can add one further recommendation. This stuff tastes good!

South End Sausage

111 Robinson Road, Salt Spring Island | 250-653-9845
southendsausage.com | IG: southendsausage

Morgain Cuddy and Ramona Reigel.

■ **What is more satisfying?** Taking a raw piece of wood and turning it into a useful, long-lasting bowl, implement, or cabinet or taking some raw pieces of meat and fat and turning them into something wonderful to eat that could be devoured in seconds? For the first part of their lives Morgain Cuddy and Ramona Reigel chose wood. Morgain spent time in house construction, and was a woodturner for many years, creating and selling salad bowls and more at the Salt Spring Saturday Market and during gallery tours. He also operated a portable sawmill business, and if he has time, you might be able to get him to build you some custom cabinets or doors. Ramona was also a woodworker who made cutting boards and salad servers, but that doesn't mean they somehow magically turned into sausage makers. Morgain had been making sausages for years with his parents in a cottage-industry style and loved all aspects of "meat manipulation" while Ramona was the production manager for many years at the Salt Spring Cheese Company. In 2021, they made their first sausages together as South End Sausage, selling the sausages strictly by advance order from a great email list and website aided by tasty photos created by their daughter Helena. They used to meet their customers at designated pick-up locations with coolers loaded with fresh sausages. They also invited people to visit the little shop they had set up in the basement of their home. Luckily the local constabulary didn't think any of this activity was suspicious. Soon enough they established a real storefront just outside of Ganges, and through the nice weather part of the year, Morgain will fire up his smoker outside the shop and do Texas-style pop-up barbecue. If you're smart, you'll order something in advance so you won't be disappointed. It could be ribs, could be chicken, maybe pulled pork . . . The extra room that the shop affords allows them to carry both shelf-stable and refrigerated products like Promise Valley Yogurt from Duncan and their "take and bake" sausage rolls. The products that go beyond fresh sausage are really special, and they're very proud of their fermented and dry-cured salami. They go through a time-consuming process of fermenting and air-drying. In the case of making something like prosciutto from a leg of locally raised pork, the curing process can take up to eighteen months. Ramona, Morgain, and their part-time workers all put in some long work days in order to ensure the highest quality of products, which they are happy and thankful that their customers appreciate.

Hornby Island Tea

Hornby Island | hornbyislandtea.com | IG: hornbyislandtea

It's a safe bet to say I put in at least a few late nights getting the manuscript of this book ready for the publisher. While I love coffee, I don't usually have any caffeine past about 4:00 PM. That's where my "I Am Refreshed" tea comes in from Hornby Island Tea. No caffeine and just three ingredients, hibiscus, orange peel, and locally grown spearmint. The tea is very refreshing, hot or cold, and doesn't provide any sort of caffeine hangover. I need to be alert to type! It's high in vitamin C and natural electrolytes to boost your energy. While "I Am Refreshed" doesn't contain any black or green tea, some of the other Hornby Island Tea blends do, but they are always augmented by locally grown herbs and flowers, like island-grown spearmint, lavender, calendula, lemon balm, and ethically foraged nettles. The black and green teas, rooibos, and other herbs are imported from direct or fair-trade sources. The ethical nature of the product is the philosophy of company owner/operator Desiree Lyver, who grew up on a family farm on Hornby Island. After earning a Diploma in Environmental Science and working in the field for a few years, she decided to focus on her passion for the environment and start up what she hoped to be a sustainable small business. Years later she's well on her way to achieving her goals, by using ingredients grown on her farm and other locally based like-minded farmers and developing close ties with family-run farms in South Africa and India. And she's established her products in many grocery and wellness stores up and down Vancouver Island.

Desiree Lyver.

Denman Island Chocolate

4321 Denman Road, Denman Island | 250-335-2418
denmanislandchocolate.com | IG: denmanislandchocolate

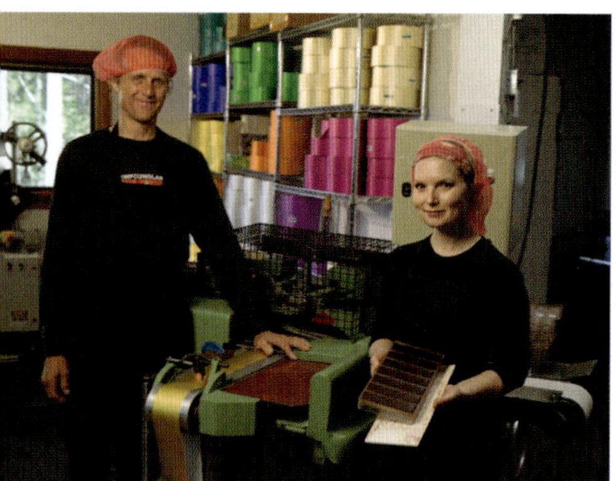

Daniel Terry and Jessica Johnston.

It's always an adventure going over to Denman Island, but the best adventure is making your way up a twisty, wooded driveway and spotting the Denman Island Chocolate factory at the top of a hill overlooking the ocean. Daniel Terry has owned this chocolate company since he started it with his wife, Ruth, in 1998. It started as a make-work project when their plans to be market gardeners on Denman in 1994 were thwarted by an overabundance of home gardeners. They had already given up on Daniel finding construction work because of an overabundance of carpenters on the island. Before they knew it, their high-quality dark chocolate bars were in great demand, and the company was born. Sadly, Ruth passed away in 2004, but Daniel maintains that he and his employees continue to make their products the way she would like them to be made. The chocolate used is all certified organic, and Denman Island Chocolate is recommended by the Food Empowerment Project to be vegan, child labour free, and slave labour free. Daniel has fun with the names of his limited-edition bars, which are a bit outside the box: Strawberry Feels, for example. Another one was Rosemary, Baby. Other than his distinctive bars with the bright foil inner wrappers poking out from their colourful labels, Denman Island Chocolate fans also look for limited-run seasonal offerings with special flavours and chocolate frogs, hearts, bunnies, Santas, and even jolly Buddhas. In 2024, Daniel decided to pass the torch on to fellow Denman Islander Jessica Johnston who will keep the legacy of high-quality organic chocolate production on the island.

Cosmo Knives

Salt Spring Island | 250-653-2435 | cosmoknives.com | IG: cosmoknives

■ **I've collected a few knives over the years**—my bread knife, my filleting knife, various paring knives, a cleaver, and a bunch of knives commonly known as chef's knives, the all-purpose sort that can be used for most chores in the kitchen, from slicing to cutting to chopping. I am always on the lookout for the next great knife, one that might feel better in my hand, keep its edge longer, or slice a tomato better, so when I heard about Seth Burton's knife-manufacturing shop on Salt Spring Island, I had to go visit. Seth's Cosmo Knives are made from scratch. He starts out with raw hunks of steel, heats them and presses them and rolls them and cuts them and grinds them and seasons them and so on until he has a finished product. In 2024, Seth introduced his signature Damascus steel blade—which in a US metallurgic study demonstrated the best edge retention of any Damascus steel tested to date in the world! These new blades have almost a snakeskin-like appearance, a little different from the traditional layered look of Damascus blades. It's not just the blades that are beautiful (and of course sharp) but the handles as well. They are often made of rosewood or maple burl and are just as beautiful as the stainless or folded Damascus steel in the blades. Since he started his business, Seth has made over four thousand knives, each individually crafted. As with many of the handmade artisanal products you'll read about in this book, his prices reflect how much work goes into each piece, the quality of the metal, the handle material. If you don't want to splurge on one for yourself, one of these knives would be a great lasts-a-lifetime gift for the foodie in your life who has everything. Oh, and if you're getting married, Seth is also in demand for his gorgeous Damascus steel and gold wedding rings. Visit his Instagram account and you'll see what I mean. Like the knives, they'll last forever.

Seth Burton.

Mouat's Housewares Store

118 Fulford-Ganges Road, Salt Spring Island | 250-537-5551
mouatstrading.com | IG: mouatshomehardware

When you live on an island, it is sometimes hard to find some of the everyday stuff you might take for granted when you live in a larger town or city. Take housewares. Well, if you live on Salt Spring Island, or maybe you're in a long-term rental for the summer, or you're just the kind of person that needs a certain thing in your short-term rental, say a stovetop espresso maker, take yourself to Mouat's Housewares Store. You can get almost anything you want there; I even found pellets for my specialty smoker barbecue. We're talking nearly four thousand square feet of retail space dedicated to housewares. This shop is part of the large Mouat's Trading building in Ganges, which includes a Home Hardware franchise, which somehow persists to this day where the hardware business is dominated by Big Box Stores. Maybe it has something to do with Mouat's being founded there in 1907 and remaining as a family-owned business all these years.

Michelle Keown, Housewares Department Manager.

Salt Spring Gelato

19C–315 Upper Ganges Road, Salt Spring Island | 250-537-1081
saltspringgelato.com

In 1994, I think people on the West Coast were just starting to get into the whole idea of what artisanal gelato was and how it could elevate you past what traditional and commercial ice creams had to offer in terms of flavour and quality. That's when Salt Spring Gelato hit the market in what was, by their own description, "a quirky little company dedicated to making top notch gelato while having fun making it." For the past fifteen or so years of their involvement with the company, Jessica Flynn and Andrew Preston are still having fun making it, but it's grown into a much larger business that distributes its gelato from Kelowna to Tofino and Victoria to Qualicum Beach. "So we cover a lot of ground," says Andrew, "and get many different flavour requests." Those flavours are many and varied, seasonal, but made with exacting precision. They note that the hardest part of the business is never seeming to have enough time. "There are no shortcuts in this business. No easy way out, no corners to cut. Everything is handmade. Everything is measured. If we could have a superpower it wouldn't be super human strength or the ability to fly. It would be adding hours to the day." Even so, as this book went to press, Salt Spring Gelato was planning another expansion. It's hard to pin them down as to their favourite products, but Andrew says Ferrero Rocher is relatively new and a big hit, while Jess favours egg nog over the holidays. And then there are the ice cream cakes. How about a two-layer cake with Belgium chocolate and salted caramel with another layer on an Oreo cookie crumble crust finished with semi-freddo and then drizzled with homemade, buttery rich caramel sauce and finished with crushed Score bars? Decadent!

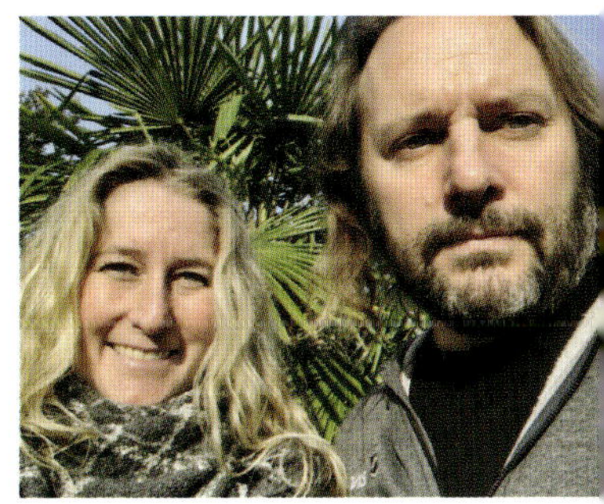

Jessica Flynn and Andrew Preston.

Salt Spring Island Cheese

285 Reynolds Road, Salt Spring Island | 250-653-2300
saltspringcheese.com | IG: saltspring_island_cheese

David Wood brought his culinary know-how with him from Toronto and started making goat cheese on Salt Spring in the mid-nineties, establishing himself as a pioneer in this area in artisan cheese making. His innovative packaging of see-through soft containers clearly shows the flavourings added to each chevre. Plain chevre sports colourful edible flowers, a thick layer of green basil leaves infuses another package, and then there are the whole slices of lemon, hot chili paste in the form of sambal ulek, and decadent white truffle paste. Salt Spring Island Cheese is also known for its feta cheeses, three Camembert-styles, and a creamy goat cheese mixed with garlic and herbs. Over the past couple of years, I've become very fond of St. Jo, the goat feta cheese made by this company. I love how it enhances the flavour of my recipe for Greek mussels. While you're on Salt Spring, visit the farm where the cheeses are made; you can walk around and watch people at work in the cheesery through large glass windows and eventually make your way to the retail store, which is full of not only all the cheeses made there (with samples for tasting) but also many different kinds of olives sold in bulk and other local preserves and artisan food products. There's a café there open from May through the fall. In my experience, it's very difficult to get out of there without several purchases that would make a very good picnic or might just get eaten in the car as you navigate the twisty roads of Salt Spring. If you can't visit the farm, you will find Salt Spring Island cheeses at the Saturday Market in Ganges and in a variety of retailers throughout the region and into Alberta and even the western US.

David Wood.

Salt Spring Seeds

250 Toynbee Road, Salt Spring Island | 250-537-5269
saltspringseeds.com | FB: Salt Spring Seeds

I met Dan Jason of Salt Spring Seeds in his garden for the first time over twenty years ago after I had received a copy of his book *The Whole Organic Food Book: Safe, Healthy Harvest from Your Garden to Your Plate*. The title alone tells you what Dan has been about for years—growing your own food and enjoying it. He's probably helped hundreds of thousands of people do that over the years by now through his seed company and his many books. Dan has been gardening since he was thirteen in his backyard garden in Montreal. He came to Salt Spring Island in 1976 and created his mail order company selling non-GMO, heritage, and open-pollinated heirloom varieties of plants and vegetables. I remember visiting his garden and seeing all the plants that were going to seed that he was going to painstakingly harvest, clean, and package. Most fascinating were the "orca" beans, an heirloom variety of kidney bean that look just like miniature killer whales with distinct black and white splotches. It was the first time I had seen something as unusual as that, and it opened my eyes to the necessity of preserving and propagating as many different kinds of plants as possible. Salt Spring Seeds offers over four hundred different products just a click away with your mouse, and you can also find them at about a dozen different shops on Vancouver Island and the Gulf Islands.

Dan Jason.

Culturalive!

Salt Spring Island | 250-653-4626 | culturalivefoods.com

■ **When I first visited Melanie Furman** in her commercial kitchen on Salt Spring Island, it was in a tiny trailer she had converted into a fully approved commercial kitchen. She was four years into making her "culturalive" sauerkrauts and kimchis for sale at the Salt Spring markets and about a dozen stores. Over ten years later, she's moved into a much larger facility and has made additions to her product line including condiments like fermented mustard and hot sauce. Melanie originally got into her food business not because she thought it was a great business idea, but because of her own experience with food. "I had a bit of a health crisis. I was working a few jobs and going to school full-time and racing back and forth from Salt Spring to Vancouver Island . . . and my system kind of crashed. I went on a few different diets and tried fermenting, and I discovered that eating fermented foods helped my body to actually digest the food as well as absorb it." I have found myself eating her two bestselling products straight out of the jar, the mild kimchi and her carrot and ginger sauerkraut. They are very fresh tasting and not too salty, and Melanie likes to use as much locally grown vegetables in her products as she can. When we last chatted on the phone, she was on her way back from Michell's Farm in Saanich with a load full of cabbage to process. While you can find her products in a list of shops found on her website, you can meet Melanie in person most Tuesdays and Saturdays when the Salt Spring Market is in season, or you can always give her a call if you want to see her fermenting operation up close.

Melanie Furman.

Monsoon Coast Trading Company

9–315 Upper Ganges Road, Salt Spring Island
monsooncoast.com | IG: monsooncoast

When I visited the production space of Monsoon Coast Trading Company, a heady aroma hit me as soon as I walked through the door of this otherwise nondescript unit in a light industrial mall in Ganges. Just a few sniffs and other worlds parade through your mind—Africa, the Middle East, and a hint of Asia, all emanating from the spice-grinding, mixing, packaging, and warehouse facility. Ironically, both current Monsoon Coast owner, Shadel Haddad, and former owner, Andrea LeBorgne, said after a while they no longer noticed the heady richness in the air when they walk in the door, but it's there all right, echoing the company slogans: Exotic World Spices, and Don't Settle For Stale. Before Shadel bought the company from Andrea, he used to sell Monsoon Coast products while managing

Shadel Haddad.

the South China Seas shop at Granville Island in Vancouver. It's where he learned about spice blends, and when a chance trip to Salt Spring revealed an ad regarding the sale of the company, he thought, *Why not?* Shadel also has culinary training—he did the food styling and developed all the recipes for the beautiful dishes you see on the Monsoon Coast website. When he is speaking to his customers, Shadel imparts his passion for creating meals from scratch with the help of his spice blends, saying the time it may take to develop a curry dish is time spent on improving yourself. I can't disagree. Shadel also offers cooking classes using his products to pass on even more knowledge. While staying true to the principles of the founder of Monsoon Coast, Doug Hall, by using only quality spices to roast, grind, and blend small batches of the product line, Shadel is also modernizing the operation with a very user-friendly website for ordering, streamlined production, and no plastic or paper bags in any of the packaging. Since taking over the company, Shadel has doubled the offerings, expanding well beyond the original South Asian focus. In my spice drawer right now? Arabian Baharat, a splendid match with lamb chops or on skewers of chicken. I also have Tunisian Harissa and Ethiopian Berbere on hand, which I love to coat potatoes or carrots with before roasting them. Monsoon Coast also offers some varieties and blends of teas. Try the Railway Chai—it really is the flavour of India in a cup.

SaltSpring Kitchen Company

319 Upper Ganges Road, Salt Spring Island | 250-931-6000
saltspringkitchen.com | IG: saltspringkitchenco

Melanie Mulherin.

I first met Melanie Mulherin of the SaltSpring Kitchen Company at the Saturday Market in Ganges. It's not hard to find half a dozen vendors there who are jam, jelly, and marmalade makers. But Melanie intrigued me with some of her novel creations, such as Pink Grapefruit & Rhubarb Marmalade and Blueberry & Basil Spread. "I develop recipes that are unique," she says, "putting things together that you normally wouldn't think of, like the pink grapefruit and rhubarb. I also try to make sure that many of my flavours will go perfectly with cheese, since we have so many great cheeses that are made here on the island." When I buy preserves rather than make them myself, I want something different. Melanie's creativity stands out in her blending of unexpected flavours and her attractive packaging. Top sellers include Spicy Tomato Savoury Spread, Raspberry & Habanero Spicy Pepper Spread, and her Candied Jalapeños—I nearly ate the whole jar of those in one sitting. Since that first meeting, Melanie's business has boomed. She's gone from making jams in her home kitchen to twenty-five different products produced in a custom-built factory complete with retail shop and tasting room. The line goes from sweet to savoury to spicy and now includes hot sauces and spreads. These products are now available in grocery stores and gift shops across the country. It's not easy to go from slaving away in your home kitchen all the way to national distribution while still maintaining the quality and originality of your product, but keeping the manufacturing close to home with a dedicated staff makes it all work. Well done, Melanie!

Salt Spring Sea Salt Ltd.

1–319 Upper Ganges Road, Salt Spring Island | 250-818-7630
saltspringseasalt.com | IG: saltspringseasalt

I remember meeting Philippe Marill not long after he had founded Salt Spring Sea Salt in 2014. The Frenchman who now called Salt Spring Island home was unapologetically proud of the fleur de sel he was making and was trying to convince as many people as possible how much flavour it could add as a finishing salt to their cooking. He wasn't wrong. The delicate flakes have a decidedly clean flavour to them but also a certain crunch that adds to your enjoyment of whatever food they are sprinkled upon. As time went on, he developed more flavours, and I was a big fan of his blackberry infused salt as it offered both a salty zip and a true BC fruit flavour. Sadly, Philippe passed away in 2022, but his long-time friends on Salt Spring, Conny Classen and Robert Steinbach, stepped in to purchase the company from his widow with the intent of preserving his legacy while moving the company forward. Conny and Robert both come from a long background in hospitality and sales, and when I talked to Conny she spoke about the challenges of taking over a small business, but she also had a pretty good idea of their goals, including getting the sales of their salt to go beyond gift shops and into more grocery stores where people will buy the salt to use it themselves, not give it away as a souvenir of Salt Spring Island. They're also developing a line of rimmer salts and getting to net zero waste by developing uses for the by-products of the salt making process. Their best compliment so far has come from a Scottish salt maker they visited so he could taste their salts, for he proclaimed their salt to be the best he had tasted . . . save his own, of course.

Robert Steinbach and Conny Classen.

Soya Nova Tofu Company

1200 Beddis Road, Salt Spring Island | 250-537-9651
soyanova.com | FB: Soya Nova Tofu Shop

■ **Soya Nova** is a collection of small buildings that houses not only owner Debbie Lauzon's home but also the commercial kitchen where the tofu is made and a room dedicated to creating her dynamite smoked tofu. Debbie started making tofu when she was living on Mayne Island forty years ago—when as a vegetarian, you couldn't just go down to the corner store and buy tofu. She had learned a bit about tofu in California. She was definitely a flower child back then, but her father called her a "blooming idiot." Her big break came when her mother gave her three hundred dollars to buy a Vitamix blender so she could grind soybeans more efficiently. That grinder is long gone but the business is still thriving. She uses up to fifteen tons of soybeans every year, and the basic ingredients she uses are simple: certified organic, non-GMO, Canadian-grown soya beans and deep well-water, unchlorinated, with a perfect 7.3 pH balance and nigari (a natural form of magnesium chloride that aids in coagulation). The product line is short and successful: Finest Medium Firm Regular Tofu; Sprouted Soybean Tofu; Westcoast Smoked Tofu; Garlic, Dill, Chili Pepper Tofu; and Zed-Spread. When she started the business back in the eighties, it was called Supernatural Tofu. But that was just when former BC premier Bill Vander Zalm was pumping Super, Natural BC, and she didn't want any political affiliations between her tofu and the BC government of the day, so she changed it to Soya Nova—Nova being her daughter's name. That's soy nice, isn't it?

Daylin Kodaly, Debbie Lauzon, and Nova Kodaly.

Woodfire Spice

500 North Road, Gabriola Island | 250-247-0095
woodfirespice.ca | IG: woodfirespice

Sharon and Chris Hooton.

First came the restaurant, simply called Woodfire, then came the spices. Chris Hooton was a chef with decades of experience in the UK, while his wife Sharon was in video production. An opportunity came up to open their own restaurant on Gabriola Island and *boom*! "The spice blends were developed in 2017," says Sharon, "after the restaurant guests kept asking why our food tasted so good. It was all due to the spice blends we were using which Chris had created himself over his forty-year career. We started by selling them in local stores on Gabriola and in Nanaimo." Now she reports they are in over a hundred stores across Vancouver Island, the Gulf Islands, and the Lower Mainland. Plus, there are US retailers, and they even fill some orders to UK fans who tasted them while visiting and love them so much. Spice rubs and blends are a competitive product line, and the marketing and outreach of Chris's inventions is one of the harder aspects of that part of their lives. But at the heart of it is creating a product that makes cooking simple. All the blending of spices has already been done by Chris, so just add to your dish and create a simple meal very easily. I like how you can buy 250-gram bags of your favourite blends so you can stick them in your cupboard to easily refill the smaller cans you can stash in your spice drawer for easy access. I'm a fan of the Coffee Chili Cocoa rub. Three of my favourite food groups ready to go in one easy can of goodness.

The Woodshed

319 Upper Ganges Road, Salt Spring Island (shop)
243 King Road, Salt Spring Island (farm stand)
250-931-7007 | woodshedprovisions.com | IG: woodshedprovisions

Haidee Hart.

■ **I first met Chef Haidee Hart** when she was the chef in charge of catering all the events and retreats at Stowell Lake Farm on Salt Spring and was impressed with her cooking style and use of produce grown at the farm and elsewhere on Salt Spring. She left Stowell Lake at the end of 2019 and had booked herself a full year of work catering events and teaching cooking classes out of the country. Then the Covid-19 pandemic hit, and all the work she had lined up disappeared. One day she was looking in a cookbook and one of the soup recipes showed the soup being stored in Mason jars. Haidee thought, *People here on Salt Spring might just go for that; make soup in jars and sell it to them.* That was the beginning of the Woodshed. Her husband fixed up an old shed on their property that was built forty years previously by his father. He found a funky retro fridge, ran electricity to it, and they filled the fridge with soup. It turned out to be a big hit. From the soup she expanded into making scones and muffins and eventually turned one of the other outbuildings on their farm into a commercial kitchen. There is still a self-serve farmstand at their farm on King Road, but eventually she moved into a new larger facility on Upper Ganges Road and has expanded even further from the soups—she makes whole meals that people can order in advance and then just pick them up and reheat them at home. There are still soups, and salads, and some baking, too, with galettes and cakes available. Not bad for a project born out of a pandemic with its humble start in an old woodshed with an old fridge.

Pacific Prowler

Centennial Dock (Ganges), Salt Spring Island | 250-221-1627
pacificprowler.ca | IG: pacificprowler

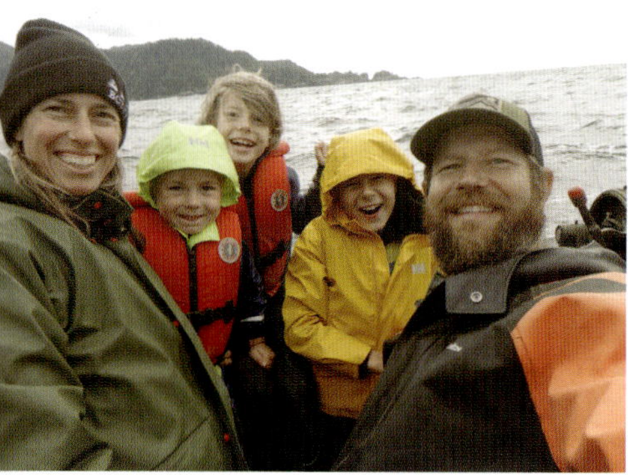

Becky Acheson, Dane Orser, and young crewmates (their sons).

■ ***Pacific Prowler*** is a trawler based out of Salt Spring Island that fishes the waters off of Haida Gwaii then returns home to sell part of their catch directly to consumers on Salt Spring, Victoria, and the Comox Valley. The *Prowler* is also the boat that Becky Acheson practically grew up on, as her father Chris was a commercial fisherman starting at age eighteen and bought the *Prowler* back in the eighties. Dane Orser, her husband, was more comfortable on a horse as he grew up on a cattle ranch in Alberta. But when they met and Becky got him out on the boat and catching his first ocean fish . . . well, he was hooked (pardon the pun). Now he has his captain's papers and Dane and Becky run the boat together. They mainly market the salmon catch direct to the consumer but also offer halibut, sablefish, and tuna from time to time. All their fish is processed and packaged on Salt Spring to help keep everything in the local economy. They offer some whole fish and some fillets in a variety of box sizes sold frozen by the pound, which is the best way to get fish because it gets processed as quickly after it is caught as possible and frozen to keep in the texture and flavour.

Quadra Island Fisheries

Quathiaski Cove, Quadra Island | 250-710-7344
quadraislandfisheries.com | FB: Quadra Island Fisheries

For Lance Underwood and Lindsay Cowan of Quadra Island Fisheries, the Covid-19 pandemic pushed them to where they are today, which is positioned as a booming direct-to-consumer seafood provider. Before the pandemic struck, almost all their catch of species like BC spot prawns and Dungeness crab was sold directly to wholesalers, many of them out of Canada, who then sold the product on to restaurants and fish markets. But when everything shut down, they had a lot of product on their hands that they needed to move, and they came up with the idea of taking orders off the internet and then delivering them to pre-determined pick-up locations. They service towns up and down Vancouver Island, all over the interior of BC and into Alberta, with some seasonal service even to Whitehorse and Watson Lake in the Yukon. They specialize in frozen spot prawn tails and live Dungeness crab, plus some custom cut albacore tuna, and they are getting into BC sidestripe and humpback shrimp. Lance says they are a bit of a harder sell since the shrimp are not as big as the spot prawns, but he maintains they have much better flavour—he's right, I've had all three, and the shrimp are a delicious and less expensive alternative to the prawns. To meet the demand, Lance and Lindsey are now buying seafood from other fishers and run another boat out of Prince Rupert. Lance says the key to their success is that they have a lot of diehard repeat customers who buy lots of product whenever they announce they're going to do a delivery run, and it's the people who live in smaller towns who are the best clients as they know how hard it is to get high quality seafood at a decent price elsewhere.

YOU MAY ALSO WANT TO TRY:

Outlandish Shellfish Guild, 657 Industrial Way, Quadra Island (250-203-1434). This group of shellfish farmers has a processing facility and pick-up depot on Quadra Island not far from the Campbell River/Quadra Island Ferry, but the farms are scattered across Quadra, Cortez, and Read Islands. The Guild offers different types of oysters, clams, mussels, and scallops.

Farm Gate Store

568 Fernhill Road, Mayne Island | 250-539-3700
farmgatestore.com | IG: farmgatestore

In the first edition of this book the space given to this entry was all about Deacon Vale Farm, a farm I called "an organic jewel, bursting with produce in the height of the season along with high-quality beef and chicken." While Deacon Vale Farm is still up and running, owners Don and Shanti McDougall now also operate the Farm Gate Store, a vital commercial operation serving Mayne Island. It's just two kilometres away from the farm, and you can still find Deacon Vale-branded products there, as the farm continues to produce all the jams, jellies, sauces, and preserves it always has. But now there are many more products in the store, including products and produce from other Gulf Islands and Vancouver Island. And in a nod to the ever-growing number of cooks experimenting with different foods, the store brings in specialty food products they can't find anywhere else on the island. There is also a bakery, a deli, selected seafood, and chef-prepared house-made foods like pastas, sandwiches, and burritos. Overseeing this end of the business comes naturally to Don, as he was also a professional chef before adding farmer to his resumé and championing the Mayne Island Farmers' Market and battling to open the Farm Gate Store on Mayne Island. It's a long story involving much bureaucratic wrangling, but all you need to know is that for almost anything you need to sate your hunger, the Farm Gate Store probably has it.

Shanti and Don McDougall.

Salt Spring Mercantile

101–2915 Fulford Ganges Road, Salt Spring Island | 250-653-4321
saltspringmercantile.com | IG: saltspringmercantile

■ **The current owners** of Salt Spring Mercantile are no strangers to the hospitality and service industry on Salt Spring, but Matt and Tasha Rissling happened to take over the business during the first real "heat dome" BC experienced in July of 2021. First problem to solve? Installing a heat pump to help cool things down. The Mercantile has been around in one form or another for over sixty years now, morphing from a general store to gas station/convenience store to grocery store with a specialty in gourmet items from not only Salt Spring Island but around the world. A commercial kitchen allows them to make sandwiches, deli items, cookies, scones, sausage rolls, and much more every day. Since they took over, the Risslings have made a fair number of cosmetic upgrades and added some much-needed storage. Matt says they're very proud of what they stock. "We have such a wonderful array of local, artisan products. For me, it's the chocolate bars from Harlan's in Ganges, the spreads from Salt Spring Kitchen, and Francis Bread Fridays are a huge hit, where our friends from the woodfired bakery in Ganges bring us a selection of loaves and pastries." It's also a real hub for locals and tourists to get staples on the south end of Salt Spring Island. "The next closest place to buy groceries is fifteen kilometres away in Ganges which makes for a thirty-k round trip for a jug of milk or a loaf of bread. Tourists love all the great local products, and on hot days, ice cream bars and cold drinks!"

The Rissling Family.

SATURDAY SOJOURN

I know that ferry rides are expensive. But don't let a short ferry ride put you off from a day trip to Salt Spring Island. Get together with a group of friends and share the cost of the ferry, but make sure you leave room in the trunk for your cameras, a cooler, and the bags of goodies you're sure to be packing on your return. The Saturday Market in Ganges is a delightful mix of arts and crafts and lots and lots of farmers and food producers. Grab a baguette from your favourite baker on-site—you'll need it later.

On the waterfront, not far from the market, you will likely find live crab for sale, and maybe some salmon or prawns depending on the time of year—this is where the cooler comes in for the first time. Don't have a pot big enough to cook the crab? Drop by the **Housewares Store in Mouat's Trading** in Ganges, where all your kitchen gear needs will be met. You may have sampled some of David Wood's **Salt Spring Island Cheese** at the market but save room for more sampling of a wider variety of his products and other tasty edibles at his farm on Reynolds Road: cheese, crackers, olives, tapenades, everything you need for a great picnic spread. Now that baguette comes into play as you head to **Ruckle Provincial Park**. Carry on past the campground to the day-use area, and you'll find picnic tables with a fine view of boats and ferries passing by as you dine on your chosen delectables.

If you are totally into knives for your kitchen, you should make an appointment to check out Seth Burton's **Cosmo Knives**. He is one of the only knife makers of top calibre in Western Canada, and he takes custom orders. By now you might want to head back to the ferry to Swartz Bay. Leave yourself enough time to have dinner at Matt Rissling's **Rock Salt Restaurant and Café**, right beside the Fulford Harbour ferry terminal. Last minute snacks for the ferry? You're right by Rissling's **Salt Spring Mercantile**, too. As you see the ferry coming in, head back to your car, check the ice in your cooler, and reflect on a day well spent as you finish it with a mini ocean cruise back to Swartz Bay.

Acknowledgements

My wife, Ramona, is ever at my side as my sounding board, my inspiration, and a willing partner in trying so many of the products mentioned in this book. The late, great James Barber was a guiding force from the time I watched him on TV on weekday afternoons as the Urban Peasant. I learned a lot about cooking from him, and when finally I met him, he encouraged me as a food journalist and an ardent lover of the bounty of the Cowichan Valley. In that same way, Chef Bill Jones of Deerholme Farm in Glenora has always shared his techniques, recipes, mushroom finds, and indulges in our mutual zeal for barbecue. I have to mention another colleague of mine, Nathan Fong, who left this world much too early. He was not only a good friend, but one of Canada's best food stylists who introduced me to so many new people, new restaurants, and new foods on our adventures shared not only in British Columbia but around the world.

Special thanks for help with this edition to Max Gimson for his invaluable research, Colin Newell for coffee company advice and some photography, and especially to Stephen Hawkins, a long-time friend and excellent photographer whose work you have seen on many of these pages. He's also been a patient mentor for me as I learned to take better photos over the years.

Suggested Reading

I'm all about sustainable production, local and organic when possible, and smart shopping.

Here are some of the books I've read over the years that have helped me develop my philosophy of using the money I budget for food.

The 100-Mile Diet: A Year of Local Eating, Alisa Smith and J.B. MacKinnon (Vintage Canada, 2007)

This is the book that has been the inspiration for many locally sourced diets, and it remains a sometimes whimsical look into the tough chore that faced Vancouver apartment dwellers Smith and MacKinnon: they started their diet in the springtime when there was barely a leaf of local lettuce to be found near their home.

The Omnivore's Dilemma: A Natural History of Four Meals, Michael Pollan (The Penguin Press, 2006)

Pollan, a professor of journalism and author of three previous books, really hit the mark with this tome that asks all the right questions about where our food comes from and how we should eat. His follow-up to *The Omnivore's Dilemma*, called *In Defense of Food: An Eater's Manifesto,* in 2008, offered this motto: "Eat food. Not too much. Mostly plants."

Bottomfeeder: How to Eat Ethically in a World of Vanishing Seafood, Taras Grescoe (Bloomsbury USA, 2008)

Montreal-based freelance writer Grescoe travelled the world to bring us the ethical lowdown on the world of seafood. He investigates many of the major species we need to be concerned about: salmon, tuna, and shrimp.

The Urban Food Revolution: Changing the Way We Feed Cities, Peter Ladner (New Society Publishers, 2011)

Peter Ladner is a former Vancouver city councillor and co-founder of the *Business in Vancouver* weekly newspaper, so he sees food in the city from a journalistic and political side. This well-researched book looks at some common myths about our food system and how we can get more local food back into our urban lifestyles.

I was first attracted to publishing with TouchWood Editions when featuring some of TouchWood's BC-specific food books on my CBC Radio show. I admired the dedication to showcasing local food and drink so here are three more books you might want to read to add to your knowledge about what amazing beverages we produce on Vancouver Island and how to best use the food ingredients that are grown here:

All the Dirt: Reflections on Organic Farming, Rachel Fisher, Heather Stretch, Robin Tunnicliffe (TouchWood Editions, 2012)

If you have ever wondered how farmers do it, or have considered getting into farming yourself, even on a small scale, this is the book for you. These farmers have done it all, through bad weather, pests, and Monsanto. Honest and forthright, it amazes you that they have been able to triumph in careers that are almost set up to fail from the start.

The Waste Not, Want Not Cookbook: Save Food, Save Money, and Save the Planet, Cinda Chavich (TouchWood Editions, 2015)

I first got to know Cinda while interviewing her about some of the previous cookbooks she produced while living in Calgary. Happily for us Islanders, she moved to Victoria and produced a cookbook that has become increasingly relevant as food prices were hit by inflation in the first half of this decade. More than 140 recipes and countless brilliant ideas for using everything up!

Island Craft, Your Guide to the Breweries of Vancouver Island, Jon C. Stott (Touchwood Editions, 2019)

The brewery landscape on Vancouver Island will continue to shift and change, but to get an excellent history of how brewing beer started here in 1858 and waxed and waned until the resurgence in craft brewing began anew in the early 1980s, pick up a copy of Stott's book. Along with the history, you'll find profiles of many of the craft breweries that occupy "top dog" billing in today's marketplace.

The Distilleries of Vancouver Island, A Guided Tour of West Coast Craft and Artisan Spirits. Marianne Scott (Touchwood Editions, 2021)

Like the craft brewing industry, the distilling industry on Vancouver Island has blossomed in recent years. Marianne Scott also delves into the history of distilling here and how today's distilleries all have an interesting backstory as to how they came into being.

Image Credits

Don Genova, p. viii, 13, 32, 35, 36, 38–39, 46, 55, 59, 61, 68, 70, 71, 72, 86, 91, 101, 113, 114, 130, 132, 133, 137, 146, 158, 162, 163, 167, 168, 170, 175, 176, 178, 182, 185, 192-193, 198, 200, 201, 202, 208, 212, 216, 222, 240, 244, 245, 247, 252.

Stephen Hawkins, p. 8, 9, 16, 30, 31, 64, 90, 131, 134, 149, 151, 152, 155, 188, 223, 226-227, 262-263.

Colin Newell, p. 56, 164, 165, 177, 181, 190

Illustrations by Sydney Barnes

Cover, Laurent Beique, Vancouver Island
Cover, Anne Preble, tomato
Cover, Nicole Holman, seaweed
Cover, Braeden Houtman, goat
Cover, Dorata Lockyer, woman and cow

ii, Jessica Ruscello
1, Laura Bicknell
2–3, Cole Freeman
4, Hendrik Schuette
11, Two Peas Photography
14, Ali Roddam
17, Mackenzie Ferns
18, Ocea Hill
20, Shantina Rae
21, Karen McKinnon
22, Ali Roddam
23, Kyle Graham
24, Brad Chappell
25, Boomer Jerritt
27, Michelle Rankin
28, Clever Crow Farms
29, Karen McKinnon
33, Lee Gibson
40, Paula Barnes
42, Midstride Technologies
47, Mark Primmer
48, Jennifer Palmer
49, Merridale Cidery and Distillery
50, Sean Fenzl
53, Sean Dalin
57, Nik West
60, Cowichan Milk Company
62, Dorata Lockyer
63, Dorata Lockyer
65, Brave Art Media
66, Adrian Fletcher
67, Cowichan Pasta Company
69, Triple Smoke Foods
74, RuneGate Studio
76, Sehii Dominov
78–79, Perry Kibler
80, Sergio Arteaga
82, Aditya Chinchure
88, Ashley Marston
93, Sharon Nesvog
94, Clover June
95, Flying Fish
96, Danika McDowell
98, Joshua Ford
99, Hannah Ashton
100, Little Qualicum Cheeseworks
102, Alan Heartfield
103, Teresa Honeyman
104, Michel Rechon-Reguet
105, The Primal Sisters
106, Nicole Holman
107, Nicole Holman
108, Alex Taalman
109, Taylor Shellfish Farms
110, Dylan Leeder
111, St. Jean's Cannery

Index

G

H

N

Q

R

S

T

Y

Z

NOTES

NOTES

NOTES

NOTES

NOTES

PHOTO BY STEPHEN HAWKINS.

Don Genova is an award-winning, Victoria-based food and travel journalist. Over the years he has contributed to newspapers like *The Globe and Mail* and *National Post*, magazines like *enRoute*, *EAT*, and *YAM*, and a great number of both radio and television columns for the CBC. He was part of the James Beard-award winning team behind Nick Versteeg's DV Cuisine Documentary on The Bocuse d'Or. Don has also been nominated four other times for James Beard Media Awards for his radio and podcast programs. Don holds a Master of Food Culture from the University of Gastronomic Sciences in Italy in 2007. He also holds a Bachelor of Environmental Science from the University of Waterloo and is an honours graduate of the Humber College Radio Broadcasting Program. Follow Don on Instagram @dongenova.

DONGENOVA.COM